How To Be Happy restores dignity to the pursuit of happiness. In a world obsessed with optimisation and performance, Declan Edwards treats happiness not as a reward for success or a personality trait, but as a set of human skills that can be learned, practised and shared. The result is a refreshingly grounded, human-centred guide that is both scientifically rigorous and genuinely useful.

Hamza Khan, author and internationally renowned keynote speaker

Grounded in science. Rich in humanity. Free of BS. *How To Be Happy* dismantles the happiness industry's biggest myths and offers something tangible: the way to a richer, fuller life.

Dr Justin Coulson, author, speaker and parenting expert

This is the book that all humans need ... and need to read. Declan's research and expertise on the subject of happiness is extraordinary and his commitment to the wellbeing of the world goes well beyond the written word. Sometimes books temporarily move you; this book guides you to be a better, happier human.

Karl Treacher, CEO at The Culture Institute of Australia

This book isn't just theory; it's a practical roadmap for cultivating happiness as a skill. Declan's ability to translate complex frameworks into actionable steps makes this a must-read for anyone seeking lasting happiness. At a time when stress and disconnection are at record highs, this book offers evidence-based strategies that can genuinely change lives. If you've ever wondered how to be happy, not just fleetingly but sustainably, this book is your guide.

Dr Megan Lee, professor at Bond University

My personal happiness strategy? Chocolate brownies. But *How To Be Happy* goes beyond the sugar high. Declan brings authenticity, humour and real-life insight to the often perplexing topic of happiness. This book cuts through wellness-washing with wit and wisdom, with practical tools for building genuine resilience. It's a clever, grounded, real-world guide to sustainable happiness. If you're sceptical of fleeting highs and happiness books, start here.

Rebecca Moulynox, GM of Great Place to Work ANZ

In a world overflowing with advice on happiness, *How To Be Happy* stands out for one simple reason: it actually helps. Declan Edwards does not sell short cuts, slogans or false positivity. Instead, he offers a grounded, evidence-based, deeply human guide to living a more fulfilling life.

What I love most about this book is the balance. Declan blends science, philosophy, personal story and practical tools in a way that feels both intelligent and accessible. You do not just learn about happiness; you also begin to understand yourself and the skills that genuinely make life better.

Knowing Declan personally, I have seen firsthand that he truly lives what he teaches. The principles in this book are not just well researched; they are also embodied. That integrity comes through on every page. This is not a book you read once and forget. It is a guide you return to when life feels noisy or uncertain, and it has the power to genuinely change how you relate to yourself and the world around you.

Sebastian Terry, author and internationally renowned keynote speaker

HOW TO BE HAPPY

STOP CHASING HAPPINESS, LEARN THE 5 SKILLS TO CREATE IT INSTEAD

DECLAN EDWARDS

WILEY

First published 2026 by John Wiley & Sons Australia, Ltd

ISBN: 978-1-394-42111-4

A catalogue record for this book is available from the National Library of Australia

Registered Office
John Wiley & Sons Australia, Ltd. Level 4, 600 Bourke Street, Melbourne, VIC 3000, Australia

For details of our global editorial offices, customer services, and more information about Wiley products visit us at www.wiley.com.

Wiley also publishes its books in a variety of electronic formats and by print-on-demand. Some content that appears in standard print versions of this book may not be available in other formats.

Internal images: ch02: Expression icons: © David/Adobe Stock; ch05: line art tree: © FARJANAAKTER/Adobe Stock

Cover design by Wiley

Set in 11/16 pts and Palatino LT Std by Straive, Chennai, India.

Contents

Introduction

At the end of 2020, a year shaped by a global pandemic, fires, wars and the upheaval of the world as we knew it, Google released its annual 'Year in Search' results and video. This video, like all the others that came before it, highlighted the most searched topics for the year. Understandably, terms such as 'Australian bushfires', 'pandemic', 'COVID-19' and 'black lives matter' ranked highly. But Google Trends also highlighted another rising search term for the year that surprised a lot of people—myself included.

In 2020, more than ever before, people searched for 'happiness'.

In some of our most globally challenging, most disruptive and most unprecedented times, people increasingly sought out answers for how they could be happier. Even today, a cursory search for 'how to be happy' elicits a little over 8 billion results—approximately one for every single person alive on the planet. Clearly, a lot of people care a great deal about happiness. Based on the fact that you're reading this book, I'm guessing you also care deeply about happiness. If so, you're not alone, and nor are you the first to be curious about what it means to live a happy life.

A (very) brief history of happiness

Humanity has wrestled with happiness for at least the past 3000 years. Ancient civilisations, from the Greeks to the Egyptians, and the Chinese to the Indians, all pondered the nature of happiness.

In India, ancient texts such as the Vedas and the Upanishads discuss the pursuit of bliss (*ananda*) through spiritual practice and self-realisation. Chinese philosophy, notably Confucianism and Taoism, also explore the concept of happiness as an expression of harmony between ourselves and the universe. Confucius believed that personal and societal harmony was essential for happiness. Laozi, the founder of Taoism, passionately advocated for living our lives in accordance with the simple and harmonious nature of the Tao (the Way).

In Ancient Greece, philosophers such as Aristotle and Epicurus explored what it meant to live a good life, emphasising *eudaemonia*—often translated as a flourishing life or wellbeing, over mere pleasure. Aristotle even went as far as to famously posit that happiness is the ultimate purpose of human existence, achieved through the cultivation of virtue and a life of rational activity. (If you find yourself nodding in agreement with this grand statement, you'll be happy to know that you will be hearing more from Aristotle and his theories on happiness later on in this book.)

Happiness also appears in the foundations of many major religions. Across Christianity, Buddhism, Islam and Hinduism, teachings often emphasise inner peace, contentment and the pursuit of higher states of happiness.

For example, the Buddhist concept of Nirvana is centred on the ultimate state of happiness, peace and liberation from suffering.

In Christianity, the Beatitudes describe blessedness, which can be interpreted as a form of happiness. The Quran frequently mentions the importance of inner peace and satisfaction. Lastly, Hinduism's concept of Moksha represents an ultimately desired state of happiness, bliss and liberation from the endless cycle of rebirth.

However, happiness hasn't just made itself known in the philosophies and faiths of our global species throughout history. Happiness is also woven into the very fabric and founding principles of modern nations.

The American Declaration of Independence famously states that the pursuit of happiness is an inalienable right. This decision by America's founding fathers underscores the value and importance that happiness holds within our collective human consciousness. This notion that happiness is a fundamental human right has gone on to further influence political ideologies and the strategic development of societies worldwide.

Bhutan, for example, measures its success through Gross National Happiness rather than Gross Domestic Product alone. In this country, leaders consider success not only in the form of economic growth but also through the lens of the wellbeing of their citizens. Indeed, as you read this book, a growing number of countries—including Canada, New Zealand, Finland, the United Kingdom and, more recently, Australia—are following suit and committing to wellbeing budgets and happiness measures.

Moving to the scientific study of happiness

Considering its lengthy history and significant impact on humanity, you may be surprised to hear that studying happiness scientifically is a relatively new pursuit. Known as 'positive psychology', the field of happiness science only began to gain notable traction within the past 50 years. Despite its relative youth as a field of science, this area of research is uncovering profound discoveries and toolkits about what it takes to live a fulfilling life.

Unlike traditional psychology, which often focuses on diagnosing and treating mental illness, positive psychology aims to enhance wellbeing and further human flourishing. This shift represents a significant evolution in the field of psychology, moving from a deficit-focused model to one that emphasises strengths and fulfilling human potential.

Researchers in positive psychology spend their entire careers diving into questions such as, 'What are the characteristics of happy people?', 'What practices can improve life satisfaction?', 'How can institutions promote wellbeing?' and, in the case of my research for this book, 'How can people be happy?'

By focusing on what makes life most worth living, positive psychology opens up new pathways to happiness, emphasising that this is not just a fleeting feeling, but a sustainable, achievable goal.

Through my work, not only as a happiness researcher but also as a personal happiness coach and workplace happiness consultant, I've seen how this approach empowers people to cultivate their own happiness. It doesn't do so through silver bullet strategies or wishful thinking, but via the practical application of strategies that are supported by scientific research. It's this approach that forms the foundation for all of the skills, tools and concepts I'm going to share with you throughout this book.

But first, let's make a return to our Google search for 'how to be happy'.

Overwhelmed by (costly) options

If you were to google 'how to be happy' now, you could easily become overwhelmed and lost among the 8 billion results. Simply through seeking higher levels of happiness in your life, you are confronted by an endless and chaotic puzzle of methods for boosting how happy you feel—with advice ranging from meditation to massages, affirmations to antioxidants, and self-care to sunning your bum hole. (I kid you not; look it up.)

While millions of people google 'how to be happy' each month, it seems almost just as many are quick to jump in with answers. Admittedly, some of the answers are fantastic; however, others are absolutely hopeless. Most of them fall somewhere in the middle. Doctors, philosophers, lecturers, teachers, allied health professionals, psychologists, coaches, therapists and alternative wellbeing practitioners are all incredibly eager to tell you their distinct recipe or path to a happier life.

The reason behind this is simple: a lot of money can be made in the industry of peddling happiness. In 2022, the global personal development industry was valued at US$43.77 billion and is estimated to be growing by 5.5 to 7 per cent per year (according to a Research and Markets report from 2023). Add in the psychology and counselling market value (US$74.6 billion in 2024, according to Kentley Insights) and suddenly a lot of money is being invested into the pursuit of happiness.

But how well is this money being invested? According to the statistics, not very well at all.

Despite our growing interest in, obsession with and spending on happiness, we don't seem to be making much progress. On a global scale, happiness has increased for the past two years (good news), but in high-income countries such as Australia, America, New Zealand, Canada and the United Kingdom, happiness is dropping—and especially among younger generations (bad news).

In Australia specifically, almost two in every five people have experienced a mental health disorder in their lifetime, and one in five people have experienced mental health struggles within the past year (according to 2023 data from the Australian Bureau of Statistics). And Gallup research from 2024 highlights that, in many countries, anger, stress, sadness, physical pain and worry are among the highest on record.

Finding hope among the chaos

In spite of statistics and trendlines like the ones just outlined, I still remain hopeful. And the reason I am hopeful is because I believe that a key reason many people don't feel happier is because they've been sold a fundamentally flawed approach to happiness. 'New happiness' philosopher Stephanie Harrison calls this flawed approach to happiness the 'old happy'. It's an approach characterised by:

- defining your value only through your accomplishments
- feeling not good enough as you are
- treating happiness as an individualistic pursuit
- endlessly needing to be better
- seeing other people as competition, not collaborators
- viewing happiness as an external and conditional milestone.

No wonder, when this is the approach to happiness we've been sold, that so many of us struggle to be genuinely happy with ourselves and our lives. Now, more than ever, we need a happiness revolution.

That's why I've written this book—for it to act as an evidence-informed, down-to-earth map and compass for your own happiness journey. This book is a culmination not only of years of academic research and study but also of my own decade-long personal pursuit of happiness.

A little bit about me

Since I'm now a happiness researcher, a lot of people think I must have always been a happy person. But that is far from the truth. In fact, what first got me into happiness research was that I had no idea how to be happy within myself.

I had no idea what happiness was, looked like or felt like—at least, not in any way that felt long term and sustainable. As a result, I spent many of my formative years, and particularly my teenage years, pursuing everyone else's idea of happiness. This led to chasing happiness through the next accomplishment and the next achievement, hoping and praying that I'd magically feel happier when I reached life's next big milestone.

I gambled my sense of happiness on nearly anything you can imagine:

- what other people thought of me
- how accomplished or successful I was
- the next holiday
- the next job
- the next promotion
- the next pay rise
- the next relationship.

All this gambling and chasing just led to a deep sense of unhappiness, lack of fulfilment and dissatisfaction. So, I began reaching out to mentors, coaches and professionals, asking for their guidance and help. I wanted to know what they knew about happiness, because I felt like I hadn't really learned a thing about happiness in school.

This journey eventually led me to complete a master's degree in positive psychology, and to study complementary fields such as acceptance and commitment therapy (ACT) and mindfulness-based stress reduction (MBSR). It also led to me travelling the world seeking insights into happiness.

The interactions I've had throughout this journey, combined with delivering over 10 000 hours of personal happiness coaching and workplace happiness consulting, have profoundly shaped me as a person. And I've been able to distil everything I've learned about happiness over the past decade into the following five core skills:

1. expanding your emotional intelligence
2. learning to look inwards
3. retraining your brain
4. knowing yourself
5. directing your life.

Whenever people ask me what it takes to live a happier life, I come back to these five skills. If I could only ever teach five things about happiness for the rest of my life, these are the five that I would choose. (I cover each of these skills in detail in chapters 2 to 6.)

I speak with full sincerity when I say that these five skills have undoubtedly made me a happier person and improved the lives of our clients at BU Happiness College. If more of us can learn them and practice them, they hold the potential to make the world as we know it a little bit happier.

How to use this book

Before we officially get started, I have four recommendations to ensure you gain the most value, insight and positive impact from each of the chapters to come.

A guidebook is not a rulebook

Think of this book first and foremost as a guidebook, not a rulebook. What's covered in the following chapters isn't an exhaustive compendium of every different strategy that can boost your happiness; nor is it a set of rigid rules you must follow. Instead, it's an opportunity for you to learn about, experiment with and ultimately choose some strategies that work for you personally. While I may be an expert in the science of happiness, I'm never going to be an expert on you or your life. That's your domain.

The toolkit is evolving

Psychology is an evolving field. What may be accurate and best practice at the time of writing might change as new research emerges. To further add complexity, researchers and academics have a frustratingly well-developed skill of proving and disproving each other's work. On top of all this is also the crisis of confidence related to how repeatable, and therefore how scientifically valid, many studies are. This academic crisis is present in multiple disciplines of research, including the psychological sciences. To my highest capabilities, I've aimed to build this book primarily around concepts and strategies that are largely agreed on and have withstood the test of time.

In saying that, I'm not the kind of guy to yuck someone's yum. I may not subscribe to astrology but I don't think that means nobody should believe in it. I believe that if you've found some tools that help you navigate life with a bit more happiness, and they don't harm anyone else, who the hell am I to say don't do that. So I wholeheartedly invite you to take what you like from the tools shared in this book, and leave the rest behind.

Knowledge is not *power*

You've likely heard the saying, 'Knowledge is power'. You may have heard it repeated in schools, workplaces and, ironically enough, countless self-help books. I'm here to tell you that, in the area of happiness and change, it's a bald-faced lie.

Knowledge is a terrible predictor of positive change. Think about it: most people know the fundamentals of eating healthily and exercising. Despite this knowledge, how many people continue to struggle with their physical health? Ask anyone you pass today about the fundamentals of good money management (aspects such as spending less than you earn) and the vast majority of people will have enough knowledge to give good answers. Yet a staggering amount of people still struggle to manage their financial wellbeing.

A giant gap exists between knowledge and change.

And don't worry – I'm not going to tell you that the gap is bridged by motivation, willpower and hustle (gross). Countless studies have shown that hustle culture doesn't lead to sustainable change either. So what's the solution?

I believe you need four things to make sustainable and positive changes in your life:

1. *Knowledge:* I know I just said knowledge is not power, but it still has a role to play in making positive changes stick. You do need to gain some basic principles, strategies, resources and tools along the way. You can have all the motivation

in the world but without any knowledge you're just going to be a motivated fool—and the world doesn't need more of them.

2. *Support:* Change doesn't happen in isolation; it happens as part of a system. Numerous studies have shown that when you have a support network in your corner, your chances of success increase dramatically. To help you out with this, I've shared some relevant case studies and personal stories throughout the book. The intention behind these stories is to demonstrate that you're not alone in the challenges you have with your mind and emotions. One of my favourite things to remind people is that we're all going through our first attempt at living. Unless you're a believer in reincarnation, the fundamental fact is that every single person you meet is having their first go at life. We're all just trying to figure it out, but I believe life is better (and happier) when we work it out together.
3. *Practice:* Mark my words: you're going to suck at some of the recommendations I make in this book. You'll struggle with them, stuff them up and say that they're too difficult. That's a good thing—it's part of learning any new skill. Nobody picked up a guitar, played for 30 minutes and then complained that they weren't Jimi Hendrix. But when it comes to the skills associated with happiness, too many people fall into the trap of believing they're either naturally gifted at it or it's not meant for them. Give yourself permission to struggle. Give yourself space to stuff it up. Give yourself a chance to practice. To help you out with this, I've included exercises and thought experiments for you to complete within each chapter.
4. *Revision:* Have you ever had a slice of pizza the next day and thought to yourself, *Mmmmm, this is even better the second time around.* (If you haven't, you're either lying or you need

to go out and try some second-day pizza leftovers ASAP.) And that's how I want you to think of this book. Don't microwave it, but do revisit it at least twice. Flick it open to a random page instead of scrolling social media one night or jump ahead to certain chapters that resonated with you. Each time you re-read a chapter, you'll either have new realisations, new takeaways and new lightbulb moments; or you'll receive a healthy reminder about a skill that may be getting a little rusty. And if you want some extra toppings to go with that second-day pizza, you can head to my website (www.buhappinesscollege.com) for extra happiness resources, tips and tools.

Action (and fun) is what matters

Lastly, considering we're about to embark on this pursuit of happiness together, I want to make a promise to you: in the coming chapters, you're going to not only learn about profoundly fascinating happiness concepts, but also gain practical, tangible and actionable steps that you can take to immediately begin enhancing your happiness. This isn't a book of concept and theory; it's a book of strategy and action.

And as impactful as I hope this book will be for you, I also deeply hope that you can have a laugh and a bit of fun along the way. Admittedly, I can't promise this one—after all, humour is subjective and you may think that my jokes are rubbish. But I'll still do my best to bring moments of levity and playfulness to what can often be exceedingly serious topics: self-help, psychology and happiness.

So with all that said and done, let's figure out an answer to that tricky little question of 'how to be happy'.

But first, we need to start with a shorter question…

Chapter 1

What *is* happiness?

You might think that with millions of people googling 'how to be happy' each month, and with millions more answering, we would have happiness nailed down by now. But we don't. Despite holding a prime position in the minds of humankind for thousands of years, happiness often feels more confusing than ever. I believe that a significant reason for this is that we can't seem to agree on what happiness actually is in the first place.

When I ask you, 'What is happiness?' what comes to mind? What words do you use to describe it? Is it a fleeting emotion, a state of being or something else entirely?

Before I dive into the theories, foundations, skills and tools outlined through the rest of this book, I first want to share something more relatable, down-to-earth and human. Since 2019, I've been asking people from all around the world that very question: 'What is happiness?' And I've been learning a lot from their answers.

My biggest takeaway is that no matter who I asked—no matter the country we were in, no matter how different each person's background and lived experience was—everyone had an answer. And, more often than not, their answers fit quite nicely within one or more of the theories, foundations and skills I share in this book.

For now, though, I invite you to consider some of the answers I've received from people around the world and reflect on how well they align with your definition of happiness.

'What is happiness?': Case studies from around the world.

Here are a handful of responses to that vital question that left a notable impression on me.

Abhimanyu (Abhi) Singh Rathore — Jodhpur, India

I met Abhi while travelling through India for three weeks in early 2023. We spoke on the ghats (riverfront steps) of Varanasi, where the city's daily rhythms of boats, bells and bodies at the water's edge made time feel layered and complex. Abhi was rebuilding his life as a professional tour guide after the COVID-19 pandemic upended tourism. For three years during the travel lockdowns, he took whatever work he could to provide for his wife, their newborn daughter and his mother. When we met, he was back on the road and on the river, welcoming travellers again.

In India, 2023 was a turning point in more ways than one. That April, the United Nations projected that India would overtake

China to become the world's most populous country. At the same time, India's rise had come with large disparities. Research from the World Inequality Lab showed a very high concentration of income and wealth at the top of society, with the top 1 per cent holding around 40 per cent of the national wealth by 2023 and over 22 per cent of income. These levels of economic concentration were among the highest globally at the time.

India wasn't only wrestling with disparities in wealth distribution, however. They were also grappling with measures of wellbeing showing an underlying base level of inequality. In the World Happiness Report 2023, India ranked toward the lower end of the global table, reflecting persistent gaps in life evaluation scores across its vast, diverse and growing population.

Against that backdrop, Abhi's work felt like a quiet antidote to abstraction. Our conversations helped me zoom back in to focus on individuals rather than getting caught up in the macro-economic big picture of societal happiness. He didn't talk with me about macro trends; he talked about faces, families and the wonder of first-time visitors seeing 'the real India'.

When I asked what happiness meant to him, he paused, looked out at the river, and told me,

> Happiness for me is either being with my family back home or being with my family of travellers on trips! To love and share my passion and to show my travellers the wonders of this beautiful country and break the myths and perception people have of India is happiness.

(continued)

His answer revealed two happiness anchors that are well supported in the research: people and place. Whether he's back home with his family or guiding his 'family of travellers', Abhi's happiness is relational in nature. And it's rooted in belonging to country, culture and heritage.

As he spoke with me, I noticed how Abhi's eyes lit up describing the moment a traveller's shoulders drop in that instant when they stop thinking about their mental image of what their trip should look like and start experiencing it in the present. It's clear that, for him, happiness isn't just personal feeling but also a shared meaning. Amid population milestones and statistical disparities, Abhi reminded me that everyday connection still changes people. Through his work, he creates small pockets where human understanding can be shared. And those pockets are often where happiness thrives.

I met Bastian and Junior Henriquez in Chile's Elqui Valley, a dark-sky haven where the night sky feels close enough to touch. A local had told me and my wife about a nearby hostel with an open mic night and musicians who would welcome a traveller with a guitar. We soon found ourselves at Olimpus Del Elqui, tucked between high-altitude ridgelines and overflowing with warmth, laughter and the gentle chaos that only hostels manage to pull off.

That night we swapped stories and jokes. We laughed about how 'Chileans don't speak real Spanish and Australians don't speak real English', and then proved that music is a universal language. Despite not speaking much English, every musician there seemed to know the lyrics to Ed Sheeran songs.

Bastian and Junior Henriquez — Valle de Elqui, Chile

Between verses, I learned more about the backstory of the brothers behind this hostel. Years earlier, Bastian and Junior had left Chile for Australia. While there, they worked and saved with a single goal: to come home and build the hostel they had imagined for years. And now here we were standing in the dream that they had built through sacrifice, persistence and care.

In 2023, as the guitars were being tuned and the crowd grabbed a meal from the outdoor kitchen, I asked each of the brothers what happiness meant to them.

Bastian told me,

> What makes me happy is sharing my knowledge, my music and my art with everyone.

(continued)

And Junior told me,

> What makes me happiest is to live each day thinking that it is the last of my life. I try to do well, help whoever I can, be a positive person and live my life to the fullest.

I could see their approach to happiness reflected in the space they had built with their hands, and in the community they had built with their hearts. It was generous, and ripe with a sense that happiness is something you pass around the room.

This is where their story could have ended. But life kept moving. When I reached out in late 2025 to ask if I could include their story in this book, Bastian told me that a lot of things had changed for them. In December, Junior was in a serious car accident and had almost died. At the same time, Bastian's mental health experienced a steep decline. He shared with me that he was navigating depression for the first time in his life.

What stood out to me most during these conversations was Bastian highlighting that he was proud of himself and his brother for seeking support. They are both receiving therapy and are on a good path. Step by step, they are healing and their happiness is returning. Inevitably, their ideas about happiness had expanded over the years. When I asked them again about happiness, Bastian now said,

> For me, happiness is recognising the balances of life. Sometimes we give too much time to one part of life and then everything else can collapse. We need to maintain balance between work, emotional wellbeing, physical health and spirituality. Keeping all of these areas of life nourished makes me happy.

> It also makes me happy to share my knowledge and the gifts that life has given me.

And Junior said,

> For me, happiness is found in the simple and unique things of everyday life. It is knowing how to enjoy both the bad moments and the good moments that life gives us. It's about valuing what you have, being happy in the now and not getting desperate for what you'd like to have in the future.

In our messages back and forth, Bastian said something in passing that stayed with me. He felt, in a way, grateful to have faced the dark. It had made him more able to recognise it in others and to sit with them when it showed up. Courage comes with that acceptance. This isn't an endorsement of suffering, but a willingness to draw meaning from it and let it soften you rather than harden you. You can bring purpose to your greatest hardships by seeing how they can help you better support others in the future.

When I think of Bastian and Junior Henriquez, I think of courage and I think of care. I still picture the courtyard of their hostel and the open mic. I see the room filled to the brim with laughter and love (and maybe a couple too many pisco sours).

I now also picture the quieter scenes that followed — the therapy appointments and check-ins with each other, the cup of maté in the morning and more balance. Their story holds two expressions of happiness: happiness as joy and happiness as care.

Their stories remind me of the importance of sharing what we have, living one day at a time, and noticing the small joys in life. I hope we are all able to honour the hard moments of life

(continued)

without letting them define us. And, just as Bastian and Junior exemplify, I hope that when darkness comes to your life, you do not go through it alone.

Bibi Han and Yong-seong Shin — Seoul, South Korea

I met Bibi Han on my last day in Seoul, with my four-month-old son tucked against my chest, my wife by my side, and three suitcases trundling behind us. I'd seen Bibi online for months. Her smile, the hugs she gave to customers and the way her cafe seemed to glow with welcome stood out to me, and I wanted to understand her happiness up close. The moment we stepped into Bibi's cafe, Hwandae Coffee Walk, we were greeted with the kind of warmth that makes you feel like a regular on your first visit. It was a small pocket of kindness in a city pulsing with pace and the endless pursuit of productivity.

Before we flew to South Korea, I'd been reading about the country's wellbeing paradox. On one hand, South Korea is a global success story. The 'Miracle on the Han River' took a war-torn nation to high-income status within a few decades. On the other hand, the country is wrestling with deep social challenges, including the world's lowest fertility rate (0.72 in 2023, with a modest rise to around 0.75 in 2024), and the highest suicide rate among all member countries of the Organisation for

Economic Cooperation and Development (OECD). These aren't abstract figures; they're signposts of strain in a culture famed for discipline and drive.

The South Korean government is slowly understanding — and acting on — these signs of strain. In 2018, it cut the legal maximum workweek from 68 to 52 hours to improve work–life balance. In December 2025, it also announced subsidies to help small firms pilot a 4.5-day workweek from January 2026 as an experiment to ease overload while protecting productivity. Government policy can't solve everything, but it can make a difference when it comes to happiness. Whether these changes will help solve South Korea's happiness crisis is yet to be seen.

And yet, inside that cafe, happiness felt disarmingly simple. When I asked Bibi what happiness meant to her, this is what she shared:

> In my view, happiness is something deeply personal. What makes me happy might not bring happiness to someone else. As a cafe owner, I find happiness in greeting people with a smile and a light hug. It's my way of sharing love and warmth with others. Of course, to some, that hug might feel uncomfortable or unnecessary, but I still believe that my way of pursuing happiness can bring a small moment of happiness to them too. I also believe that good feelings help make good coffee. The good energy we share through our smiles and hugs becomes good coffee and brunch for our guests. I truly hope people feel that when they visit.

(continued)

And her colleague Yong-seong Shin told me:

> I value everyday happiness the most! I try to notice the subtle changes that happen within my daily routines — the conversations I have with people I meet that day, or the way the weather feels. Running a cafe, I stay in the same space every day, yet I live different lives through the many guests who come and go. Through this, I hope I can become a small piece of happiness in someone's day. And when my guests are happy, I become happy too — just like in this conversation right now.

I left South Korea with a timely and important reminder. Yes, systems matter. Laws, societal norms, policies and economics all shape happiness. But Bibi and Yong-seong reminded me of the agency we all have to play our own little parts in spreading a happiness ripple effect. (More on this ripple effect later in this chapter.) We can all nurture happiness in simple day-to-day acts, such as noticing the weather on your skin, greeting someone like they belong or offering a cup of something that is even more heartwarming than coffee — care.

In their words and actions, Bibi and Yong-seong showed me how small, daily choices become sparks. They showed me how personal kindness can soften hard statistics. And they showed me that even amid a national (and global) wrestle between success and strain, we can each play our part in making the day a little lighter for someone else.

When I reflect on the answers from these case studies, alongside all of the other answers I've been fortunate enough to collect through the years, what stands out to me is that regardless of how different we may all be, each and every one of the 8 billion human beings on this planet wants the same thing: happiness.

The other thing that struck me and left a lasting impression is that we often share some universally common approaches to achieving happiness. We may express it in different ways, but the core aspects and experiences of happiness are remarkably similar. They all tend to follow at least one of the following five happiness foundations:

1. Happiness is an emotional umbrella term.
2. Happiness is a balance of pleasure and meaning.
3. Happiness is a six-ingredient recipe.
4. Happiness is *not* a destination.
5. Happiness is a skill.

Happiness is an emotional umbrella term

When we talk about happiness, we often imagine a fleeting moment of joy, like the burst of laughter from a good joke or the satisfaction of biting into a delicious piece of chocolate. But happiness is much more complex than that. It's not just a single, fleeting emotion; instead, it's an umbrella term that encompasses a wide range of feelings. To understand this better, take a look at the Feelings Wheel, shown in the following figure.

The Feelings Wheel (overleaf), developed by Dr Gloria Willcox in 1982, is a tool designed to help individuals identify and articulate their emotions. As shown in the figure, it's divided into several segments, each representing a core emotion, such as happiness, sadness, anger or fear. If you've seen the Disney movie *Inside Out*, you'll be familiar with these core emotions—they form the basis for the characters that live in the head of the main character, Riley.

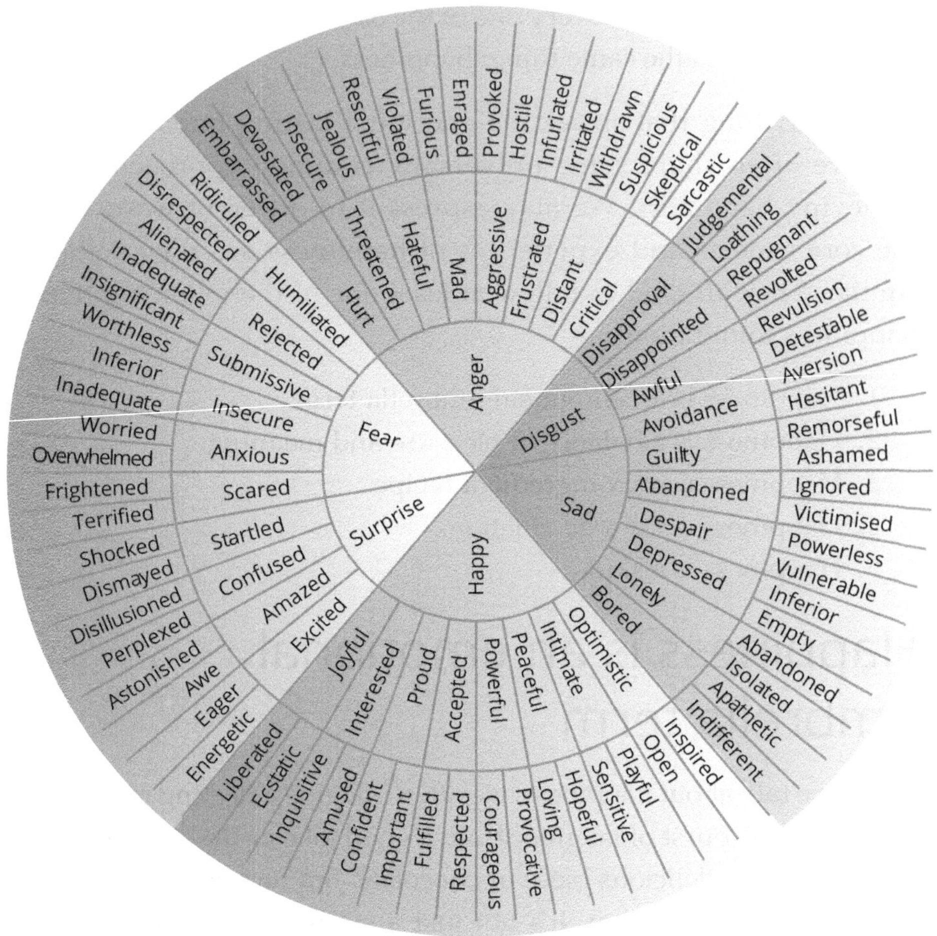

The Feelings Wheel

Each of these core emotions have more specific feelings that fall within them. For example, under 'happy', you will find emotions such as playful, proud and peaceful. This allows us to expand our scope of happiness by thinking of this core emotion as a big umbrella that includes all these other 'pleasurable' feelings.

I encourage you to get curious about your experiences of happiness. When you say you're happy, what do you really mean? Are you feeling content because you just finished a productive day at work? Or maybe you're feeling proud because you achieved a long-term goal? Perhaps you're simply interested by a funny video you saw online. Each of these emotions falls under the broader category of happiness but offer a different experience of happiness.

I'm a huge advocate for expanding your perception of happiness, because it allows you to challenge the notion that happiness only exists as a constant state of euphoria or an unending stream of 'positive vibes'. This common misconception sets you up for unrealistic emotional expectations, and ultimately results in disappointment. Real-life happiness is more nuanced and multifaceted. Sure, it includes moments of joy but it also encompasses deeper feelings of contentment and satisfaction that persist even when life doesn't go perfectly to plan.

Don't just take my word for it, though—let's put it to the test. Think about a recent time when you felt truly happy. Was this feeling based on a brief flash of joy, a fleeting feeling of pleasure, or on something deeper and more complex? Chances are, the feeling was different emotions coming together to create a deeper feeling of happiness—kind of like a cocktail of emotions that you then called 'happiness'.

Consider, for example, the happiness that comes from personal achievements. This happiness doesn't just come from the moment you cross the finish line of a race. It also comes from the purpose you feel after months of training, the pride in pushing through obstacles, and the joy of celebrating with friends and family afterward. Each of these emotions contributes to your overall sense of happiness.

Throughout the rest of the book, when I talk about 'happiness' I encourage you to think of it as more than just a fleeting feeling and to consider it through the lens of this emotional umbrella. Or think of it as a 'happiness cocktail', if that takes your fancy more.

Reflection and application

So, how can you use the Feelings Wheel to better understand and explore happiness? Start by identifying a moment when you felt happy and then break it down using the happiness section of the Feelings Wheel. Ask yourself:

- 'What emotions under the happiness umbrella do I feel most connected to?'
- 'What emotions under the happiness umbrella do I not yet understand?'

Next, choose two of the happiness emotions to explore more deeply. How would you describe them to a child? What are the differences between them?

By using the Feelings Wheel, you can gain a more nuanced understanding of what happiness means to you. This can help you recognise that happiness is not a single, fleeting emotion but a rich tapestry of interconnected feelings. This deeper understanding allows you to better appreciate the full spectrum of happiness and experience it in all its forms.

Next time you reflect on your happiness, remember that it's okay if it doesn't always feel like a burst of joy. Sometimes, it's the quiet contentment, the proud moments or the light-hearted laughs that make up the beautiful mosaic of a happy life.

Hedonia versus eudaemonia: The two distinct categories of happiness

Now that we've taken a closer look at just how layered and complex happiness can be, it's time to explore one of the most useful distinctions that philosophers and psychologists make when it comes to our experience of happiness: the difference between hedonia and eudaemonia.

This distinction dates all the way back to Ancient Greece. Hedonia, drawn from the Greek word *hēdonē*, is centred on pleasure. It creates the kind of happiness that comes from enjoyment, comfort and the absence of pain. Aristippus, one of Socrates' students, was one of the earliest proponents of this idea. He believed the ultimate goal in life was to maximise pleasure and minimise discomfort—and honestly, who can blame him? A bubble bath and a bar of chocolate go a long way.

Eudaemonia, on the other hand, comes from the Greek *eu̯dai̯monía*, meaning 'good spirit' or 'human flourishing'. This concept is most closely associated with Aristotle, who argued that real happiness—true wellbeing—comes from living a life of virtue, purpose and deep alignment with your values. For Aristotle, happiness wasn't a fleeting emotion. It was a way of being.

Let's break them down a little further.

Hedonia: The pursuit of pleasure

Hedonic happiness is what most people think of when they hear the word 'happy'. It's the kind of happiness that bubbles up when you sip your favourite coffee, get that much-needed massage, smash a goal at work or laugh with friends until your sides hurt. It's about pleasure, satisfaction and enjoyable experiences.

Absolutely nothing is wrong with this kind of happiness—in fact, it's necessary. Life without moments of pleasure and joy would feel dull and heavy. And research backs this up: hedonic wellbeing has been associated with lower stress, better physical health and greater emotional resilience.

Building and nurturing hedonic happiness can involve:

- *Indulging in sensory pleasures:* This might include activities that stimulate the senses, such as eating your favourite foods, listening to music or enjoying a spa day.
- *Seeking novelty and excitement:* This could be trying new experiences, travelling to new places or engaging in adventurous activities.
- *Focusing on achievement and accomplishment:* This includes getting a pay rise or a promotion, achieving a big goal or buying something nice for yourself.

These all boost dopamine and drive a momentarily pleasurable experience of hedonic happiness.

Eudaemonia: The pursuit of meaning

Eudaemonic happiness runs deeper. It's the sense of meaning you feel after volunteering for a cause you care about. It's the satisfaction that comes from mastering a new skill or growing as a person, or knowing you're living in a way that's true to your values. It's the deep satisfaction from nurturing relationships. Eudaemonia is less of a high than hedonic happiness, and more of a grounded, lasting sense that your life matters—to you and to others.

Building and nurturing eudaemonic happiness involves choosing activities that contribute to personal growth, meaningful connections, a sense of purpose and your values, as follows:

- *Pursuing personal growth:* Engaging in activities that promote self-improvement and personal development can lead to eudaemonic happiness. Such activities might include pursuing education, learning new skills, or setting and achieving long-term goals. Dedicating time to learn a new language or instrument, for example, not only provides a sense of accomplishment but also enhances your capabilities and broadens your horizons.
- *Building meaningful relationships:* Forming deep and lasting connections with others is a key component of eudaemonic wellbeing. This includes nurturing friendships, family bonds and romantic relationships. Meaningful relationships provide support, love and a sense of belonging. Spending quality time with loved ones, having meaningful conversations and supporting each other through challenges are all ways to build these relationships.
- *Contributing to something greater:* Eudaemonia is often found in contributing to causes that are bigger than yourself. This can be through community service, volunteering or working towards a cause that aligns with your values. Helping others and making a positive impact on your community not only benefits those you help but also gives you a profound sense of purpose and fulfilment. For example, volunteering at a local shelter or participating in environmental conservation efforts can foster a deep sense of satisfaction and purpose.
- *Living in accordance with values:* Aligning your actions with your personal values and ethical principles is crucial for eudaemonic happiness. This means making decisions and

taking actions that reflect your beliefs and morals. When you live authentically and stay true to your values, you experience a sense of integrity and coherence in your life. For instance, choosing a career that aligns with your passion and values, even if it's less lucrative, can lead to greater long-term satisfaction and happiness.

Balancing hedonia and eudaemonia

Here's the important bit when considering hedonic pleasure versus eudaemonia: happiness doesn't ask us to pick one. It doesn't say only seek pleasure or only seek purpose, but instead invites us to integrate both.

Think of hedonia and eudaemonia as the two wings of a bird. If you flap only one, you'll end up flying in circles. But together? That's how you soar.

A fulfilling life balances the thrill of joy and the depth of meaning and contentment. You can savour a glass of wine (hedonia) and also find purpose in parenting, activism or creative expression (eudaemonia). In fact, many of the best moments in life combine both. Think of laughing with someone you love—that's joy, anchored in connection.

So rather than pitting these two types of happiness against each other, aim to find your own balance. Some people lean more toward one than the other, and that's okay. The real question is what's your blend?

The next foundation explored in this chapter is, in my opinion, the best recipe we currently have for cultivating both hedonic and eudaemonic happiness. But before we dive into that, take a few minutes to reflect on this balance for yourself. Once you know what lifts you (hedonic happiness moments) and what grounds you (eudaemonic happiness moments), you can begin to build a life that does both.

Reflection and application

To explore your own balance of hedonia and eudaemonia, consider the following questions:

- What activities bring you immediate joy and pleasure?
- What pursuits give your life meaning and purpose?
- How can you incorporate both types of happiness into your daily life?
- Reflect on a recent experience of happiness — was it more hedonic or eudaemonic?
- If you were to make a perfect happiness cocktail, what's the blend of hedonic and eudaemonic happiness you would use? Would you choose a 50/50 happiness blend, or 60/40?

The PERMAH model: Six key ingredients of happiness

At this early stage of understanding the foundations for how to be happy, I want you to imagine the possibility of a scientific and evidence-based recipe for living the most fulfilling life possible. Well, guess what? You don't need to keep imagining, because this recipe exists. It comes from the modern realm of positive psychology, and specifically via the great work of Dr Martin Seligman. Known as the PERMAH model, this evidence-based recipe of six key ingredients has been shown to help people pursue, and achieve, far more fulfilling lives.

Here are the six ingredients of the PERMAH model:

1. positive/pleasurable emotions
2. engagement and flow
3. relationships
4. meaning and purpose
5. accomplishment and achievement
6. health.

Let's explore each of these ingredients.

Positive/pleasurable emotions

I'll be honest: I'm not a fan of the term 'positive emotions'. All of our emotions have a purpose and a place in our lives and labelling your emotions as 'positive' and 'negative' tends to lead to a lot of repression and emotional avoidance.

This is why I prefer to adjust the P in PERMAH to 'pleasurable emotions'. This ingredient then refers to all the emotions under the happiness umbrella term that feel genuinely good to experience. Emotions such as joy, excitement, fun, playfulness and humour can all contribute to your overall sense of emotional pleasure and form the first step in the PERMAH recipe for happiness.

Now, if you're anything like me, you may be thinking, *So if I want to feel happier in life, I need to feel more pleasurable emotions?* Seems a little 'no shit, Sherlock' doesn't it?

I thought the same thing when I learnt about this. But over time I've come to appreciate that the beauty of this component of PERMAH lies in its simplicity. After all, how easy is it to get caught up in the busy-ness and seriousness of life and forget to do things that help you to feel good? You might recognise the pleasurable emotions, but how often do you create space for them in your day-to-day life?

Reflection and application

To help you reconnect with the pleasurable emotions aspect of PERMAH, consider the following:

- When did you last laugh so hard that your tummy hurt or your eyes watered?
- When did you last feel playful and lighthearted?
- In the words of Marie Kondo, 'What sparks joy in your life?'
- How can you create more space in your day-to-day life for little moments of pleasure?

Engagement and flow

When was the last time you were so absorbed in an activity that you lost track of time? This state of complete immersion and focus is what positive psychology refers to as 'flow'. Now, if you're picturing a monk meditating on a mountain top or a surfer riding the perfect wave, you're on the right track. But flow isn't reserved for extraordinary experiences. It can also happen during everyday activities, such as painting, writing, solving a complex problem at work or gardening.

Flow occurs in that sweet spot where the challenge of the task perfectly matches your skills. It's like playing a video game that's just hard enough to keep you on your toes but not so hard that you want to throw the controller through the window. When you're in flow, you're not thinking about anything else. The worries and distractions of everyday life fade away, and you're fully engaged in what you're doing.

And here's the kicker: flow isn't just about the activity itself. It's also about the deep sense of satisfaction and fulfilment you get from being completely present.

Finding your flow requires a bit of exploration and self-awareness. You need to discover what activities draw you in and captivate your attention. Think back to times when you were so involved in something that hours felt like minutes. What were you doing? What were the conditions that helped you achieve that state?

Engagement isn't about always being in a state of flow—let's be real, life's responsibilities won't allow that. But by identifying and nurturing the activities that draw you in, you can add a deeper level of satisfaction and happiness to your life. So go ahead and find your flow.

Reflection and application

To help you connect with the engagement and flow aspect of PERMAH, reflect on the following:

- When did you last lose track of time doing something you love?
- What activities challenge you just enough to keep you fully engaged?
- How can you incorporate more of these flow-inducing activities into your daily routine?

Relationships

If you look back on the interviews and stories shared earlier in this chapter, you likely notice a common theme emerging: happiness often involves other people. Relationships, with all their complexities, are a significant part of what makes life rich and fulfilling.

I often joke that if you want a simple life, the best path is to become a hermit in the forest, free from the chaos and challenges that other people bring. Because let's face it: people inherently add complexity to our lives. This complexity can be chaotic, challenging, overwhelming and even frustrating at times. But it can also be incredibly beautiful, deeply connecting and a fundamental part of our happiness.

In fact, the longest-running study on happiness, the Harvard Study of Adult Development (led for over 20 years by Professor Robert Waldinger), has found that the number one contributor to health and happiness later in life is the strength and quality of our closest relationships. This study underscores that our connections with others are vital to our wellbeing.

I believe that relationships are one of the most underutilised, under-discussed and undervalued aspects of the PERMAH model. In the world of self-help, even the term 'self-help' implies that this journey is something you must undertake alone. But that's not the case. When considering the PERMAH model, recognising the role other people play in your life and happiness is crucial—as is the role you play in the happiness of those around you.

Reflection and application

To help you reflect on your relationships, consider these journal prompts:

- Who are the people in your life that you are deeply grateful to have?
- What would it look like to prioritise relationships and connection a little more in your life compared to what you do now?
- How can you show up as the best version of yourself in these relationships, and be mindful of the impact you have on the happiness of those around you?

Meaning and purpose

What is the purpose of life? It's a pretty big question, isn't it? Thankfully, it's not a question you have to answer in a single sweeping declaration. Instead, when considering meaning and purpose within the context of happiness and the PERMAH model, you can focus on experiencing moments that carry significance beyond themselves.

Let me share a story to illustrate this. A few years ago, a video went viral featuring William McRaven, a retired US Navy Admiral and former Navy SEAL, who explained why he made his bed every morning. He said that even if the rest of the day went terribly, at least he'd have achieved one good thing for himself. Making his bed brought a sense of order and completion, providing a small but significant anchor of purpose in his daily routine.

For McRaven, this simple act was imbued with meaning. It wasn't just about a tidy bed; it was a way to start the day with a win, creating a ripple effect of positive energy. Now, here's the beauty of meaning and purpose, and indeed any of the components of the PERMAH model: you get to decide how they fit into your life.

I'll admit that, I tried making my bed every morning for two weeks after watching that video. Much to my wife's chagrin, I felt no profound sense of purpose afterwards. To me, making the bed seemed pointless since I'd just mess it up again at night. And that's okay. The key is to find what actions or habits bring meaning and purpose to your life.

Meaning and purpose can be found in various aspects of life, from small daily routines to grand overarching goals. It's about identifying behaviours or habits that connect you to something greater than yourself.

Of course, you can expand this concept to contemplate the broader purpose of your existence. What are your beliefs about the purpose of life? Many people find answers to these big questions through their impact on others, religion or spirituality. Whether through volunteering, mentoring or simply being a good friend, connecting with a larger purpose can significantly enhance your happiness.

Reflection and application

Use the following to help you explore meaning and purpose in your life:

- What are the small, daily activities that bring a sense of meaning and purpose to your life?
- How can you prioritise and incorporate these meaningful activities into your routine?
- What are your overarching beliefs about the purpose of your life, and how can you align your actions with these beliefs?

Accomplishment and achievement

Here's something I know to be deeply true about human beings: we have this ingrained desire to feel like we're progressing, growing and achieving things in life. It feels good to feel like we're doing good. However, when it comes to accomplishment, many people make the mistake of pursuing achievements that don't actually matter to them. They chase after goals set by others or those that society deems important, rather than what truly resonates with them.

Through the lens of positive psychology and the PERMAH model, I'd encourage you to think about accomplishment and achievement from a deeply personal perspective. What feels like an achievement to you? Why is that particular accomplishment important to you as an individual?

A great way to tap into this personal perspective is through goal setting. Research shows that people who are happier and more fulfilled tend to have clear goals and milestones. These goals, however, need to be personally relevant. So you're not just setting any goal, but setting goals that align with your values and passions.

Another crucial aspect of accomplishment is celebrating your achievements. How often do you chase the next big thing, only to reach it and immediately move on without acknowledging your success? Chances are, you gloss over your achievements and dive straight into the next challenge. A big part of happiness is learning how to navigate the challenging moments and marinate in the good ones. Yet, too many of us do the opposite: we stew on the challenges and rush through our victories.

Reflection and application

To help you connect with the accomplishment and achievement aspect of PERMAH, think about the following:

- What feels like an accomplishment to you? Think about what lights you up and makes you feel like you've achieved something. This is deeply personal and varies from person to person.
- What are some goals that align with your definition of accomplishment? Consider both short-term and long-term goals. What would you like to work towards that would give you a sense of achievement?
- How can you celebrate yourself when you achieve your goals? Instead of glossing over your successes, think about how you can take a moment to be proud of yourself. What would celebrating your achievements look like?

Health

Last but not least is the sixth component of the PERMAH model and the final ingredient in positive psychology's recipe for happiness: health. When this recipe for happiness was originally written, health wasn't included; however, as more research has emerged, academics and scientists have increasingly found that our physical health and wellbeing dramatically impacts our mental and emotional health. Until we reach some dystopian future where we can separate our mind from our body, our physical health will always play a significant role in our overall sense of happiness.

When I talk about your body having a role in happiness, I'm not referring to what it looks like. What I care about here is your overall sense of physical health and wellbeing. I think of it through the lens of the 'big three': movement, nutrition, and rest and recovery.

Here's how these three elements combine to influence your physical health:

1. *Movement:* Regular physical activity is crucial for maintaining physical health. Whether through sports, going to the gym, dancing or any other form of exercise you enjoy, moving your body frequently can boost your mood, increase your energy levels and improve your overall wellbeing.
2. *Nutrition:* Eating a balanced diet that is both nourishing and enjoyable is another cornerstone of physical health. Consuming a variety of foods mindfully and staying hydrated can significantly affect your energy levels, mood and overall health.
3. *Rest and recovery:* Prioritising good-quality sleep and allowing your body to rest and recover is essential. Sleep is when your body heals and rejuvenates. Without it, your mental and physical health can suffer.

I genuinely believe that if you're moving your body frequently in ways that you enjoy, eating foods that are nourishing and enjoyable, and prioritising good-quality sleep and downtime, you'll see a dramatic improvement in your mental and emotional wellbeing. At BU Happiness College, we often say that the foundations for a happier and healthier brain start with a happier and healthier body.

Reflection and application

To help you start improving your physical health, reflect on the following:

- Of the three core aspects of physical health (movement, nutrition, and rest and recovery), which ones do you do quite well and which do you want to improve?
- What would it look like to improve on your physical health? What are some ways you can strengthen and prioritise these aspects in your life?
- Who can you turn to for support and help in these areas? Reflect on the people and resources available to you. This could include professionals such as nutritionists or personal trainers, or friends and family who support your pursuit of better physical health.

Considering all six PERMAH ingredients

To bring our exploration of the PERMAH model as a six-ingredient recipe for happiness to a close, I'd encourage you to give yourself a score out of five for each of the six components.

Which aspects of PERMAH are you doing quite well in? Which aspects could use some more love and attention? Your answers to these questions will help to guide your sense of direction when applying the happiness skills explored throughout the remainder of this book.

The Hedonic Treadmill: Mistaking happiness as a destination

The previous sections outline three happiness foundations to work with:

1. Happiness is an emotional umbrella term.
2. Happiness is a balance of pleasure and meaning.
3. Happiness is a six-ingredient recipe.

In this section, I want to warn you about the most common trap people can fall into when it comes to living a happier life: the hedonic treadmill. This psychological pitfall can be summarised in four words: 'I'll be happy when … ' For example, 'I'll be happy when I':

- make more money
- change jobs
- lose weight
- start dating someone
- leave this relationship
- have kids
- finish the renovation
- pay off the mortgage
- take a holiday
- get to the weekend.

You can insert whatever you want to complete the sentence. Whatever your answer, it leads you towards the same psychological trap of believing that happiness is a destination.

The hedonic treadmill, also known as hedonic adaptation, reveals the danger of such thinking. This theory describes the tendency of humans to return to a relatively stable level of happiness, despite major positive or negative events or life changes. In essence, we quickly adapt to our new circumstances, and the initial boost of happiness we get from achieving a goal or acquiring something new tends to fade, leaving us seeking the next thing to bring us joy.

Imagine running on a treadmill. No matter how fast you run or how far you think you've gone, you're essentially in the same place. This is what happens when you base your happiness on external achievements and acquisitions. You may think you'll be happier after the next promotion, the next purchase or the next milestone, but once you reach it, the satisfaction is fleeting.

The hedonic treadmill is a significant barrier to true happiness because it keeps you in a constant state of wanting and dissatisfaction. When you focus solely on the 'I'll be happy when' mentality, you fail to appreciate the present moment and the intrinsic joys that come from within. This perpetual chase for external validation and achievements can lead to chronic dissatisfaction and a never-ending cycle of desire.

Based on this, you may be wondering, 'Is it even possible to become happier?' Thankfully, the answer is yes. But if you want to cultivate lasting, sustainable and authentic happiness, you need to change your strategy. You can no longer gamble your happiness on the next milestone, the next material possession or the next external change.

Instead, you need to shift your focus from external achievements to internal fulfilment. Over my years of studying happiness, I've come to believe that happiness is not a destination, but a series of skills.

Reflection and application

Don't gamble your wellbeing on a finish line and the trap of 'I'll be happy when ... ' Use this quick check-in to shift attention from external results to internal rewards you can cultivate today:

- List one to three external goals you're chasing (for example, buying a house, getting promoted or running a marathon).
- For each goal, name the intrinsic feelings you hope that goal will bring you (for example, security, pride, freedom, belonging or mastery). You can use the Feelings Wheel from earlier in this chapter to help with this step.
- Come up with two ways to strengthen those feelings now while you pursue the goal.

Say your goal is buying your first house. The intrinsic feelings you might be hoping the goal will bring you and short-term actions to strengthen those feelings now might be:

- *Security and safety:* Set up an emergency fund auto-transfer, or create a simple home safety or community plan.
- *Ownership and control:* Run a weekly 20-minute 'money date' (with your partner or yourself) to review spending and savings, or create a small 'home base' corner where you live now.
- *Accomplishment:* Track one meaningful win each day and share it with a friend.

To help make this stick, try the following:

- Replace 'I'll be happy when ... ' with 'I can feel *[intrinsic reward]* today by *[action]*'.
- Celebrate process wins (effort, consistency, learning), instead of only external outcomes.

Remember — small, repeated practices can create the feeling you're chasing long before the trophy arrives. And this reduces the likelihood of you getting stuck on the hedonic treadmill.

Happiness is a skill

Whenever people ask me these days to answer the question, 'What is happiness?' my answer is, 'Happiness is a skill'. Or, more accurately, 'Happiness is a series of skill sets'.

Previously, the skills of happiness were often labelled as 'soft skills'. I personally don't use this term because it devalues these skills and undermines how challenging they are to master. Instead, I call them 'human skills' — because in a world of artificial intelligence, machine learning and robotics, these skills don't just make us happier but also help us become better human beings.

What excites me most about this foundation and approach to happiness is that it highlights the fact that happiness is something we can learn about, practise and improve on. With enough time, patience, support, resources and practice, you can learn to better manage your mind, master your emotions, and enjoy a much happier and more fulfilling life.

Knowing that happiness is a series of skills also gives you permission to stuff up along the way. The aim with each of the five skills I dive into in the following chapters, as with any skills in life, is to improve on them — not necessarily to be perfect at them. I've never met someone who decided they wanted to play basketball, shot the ball once, and then gave up because they weren't immediately scoring like Michael Jordan. People know that when they're learning a skill like basketball, they're going to struggle at first. They're going to make mistakes but eventually they will get better. I'd encourage you to take a similar approach when it comes to strengthening the happiness skills we will work on through this book.

In fact, the process of improving your happiness skills (or any skills for that matter) will likely follow a predictable four-stage pattern:

1. *Unconscious incompetence (aka ignorance is bliss):* At this stage, you don't know what you don't know. You're unaware of your lack of skill and, therefore, you don't feel the need to improve. This stage is like a child trying to ride a bike without realising they need to balance.
2. *Conscious incompetence (aka the sucky bit):* This stage is where you become painfully aware of your shortcomings. You recognise what you need to learn and improve, which can be frustrating and challenging. It's the moment you realise riding a bike isn't as easy as it looks, and you start falling a lot.
3. *Conscious competence (aka getting the hang of it):* At this point, you've acquired the skill but still need to think about it actively. Performing the task well still requires concentration and effort. It's like riding a bike and needing to focus on balancing, pedalling and steering all at the same time.
4. *Unconscious competence (aka an embodied skill):* Finally, the skill becomes second nature. You can perform it effortlessly without conscious thought. Riding a bike feels as natural as walking, and you don't need to think about balancing or pedalling anymore.

Taking this approach to happiness also explains why so many people struggle to be happy. To put it simply, they've never been taught the skills required to live a happy life. They've never had the support or resources to move out of stages two and three in the preceding skill-development model.

Think about it: our entire education system is built around the technical skills required to make you a good employee, not the human skills needed to become a happy and thriving human being.

If you didn't learn these skills at school, then hopefully you had the chance to learn them from your parents at home. But whenever I ask a room full of people to put their hands up if they felt they had highly emotionally intelligent parents who could teach them about skills such as empathy, resilience or goal setting, a shockingly low number of hands go up.

So, if the majority of people don't learn the skills of happiness at school or at home, what hope do we have in creating a happier world?

This is why I've written this book. Firstly, I want to help people embrace the concept that happiness is a skill. Secondly, I want to share my five most important skills when it comes to being happier. And, finally, I want to impress on you how much, now more than ever, your happiness matters.

I don't say it lightly when I tell you that your happiness matters now more than ever. Nor do I say it lightly when I tell you that by learning the skills in this book and improving your own happiness, you'll be playing a part in making the world a little bit happier.

People often make the mistake of thinking that it's selfish for them to focus on growing their own happiness. However, I would argue that becoming the happiest, best version of ourselves is the greatest gift we can give our loved ones, our workplaces and our communities. Becoming happier versions of ourselves has a positive impact not only on our lives but also on the lives of those around us, thanks to a phenomenon known as the 'ripple effect of happiness'.

Science has shown that happiness, like many other emotions, is contagious. In fact, according to research by Nicholas Christakis and

James Fowler, it's contagious up to three degrees of separation. Take a moment to think about what that means: if your neighbour's best friend's cousin is happier, you are likely to also be happier. I truly believe that, when applied, this communal ripple effect of happiness has the potential to make the world a happier and better place.

Research also shows that happy people are more generous than unhappy people. They are more likely to engage in positive acts that contribute to the happiness and wellbeing of those around them. They are also more creative, more innovative, more adaptable and more resilient in the face of challenges. A huge range of benefits come with being a happier version of ourselves—so many that happiness researcher Shawn Achor coined the term 'the happiness advantage' to capture just how advantageous and beneficial it is to be happy.

Being genuinely happy is a superpower. To put it simply, when we feel good, we do good. We make better decisions, perform kinder actions and create lasting positive impacts. Your happiness sparks further happiness in others. With too many people living lives of unhappiness, I believe that true, genuine, authentic happiness is the world's most untapped and underutilised resource. This is why I feel incredibly grateful that you're reading this book. I feel honoured to play my part in your happiness journey.

Because I know three things:

1. The world desperately needs more happy people.
2. I can't grow global happiness alone—this has to be a communal effort.
3. When you learn the skills of happiness, you'll automatically create your own happiness ripple effect.

With these three things in mind, let's learn the five most crucial skills behind 'how to be happy'.

Chapter 2

Expanding your emotional intelligence

The first skill of happiness

Emotions—they can be pesky little things. They come and go as they please, often overstaying their welcome like an uninvited house guest.

This is how many of us view our emotions—as nuisances or things that get in the way. And, as a result, we wrestle with our emotions. All too often, we fall into the dangerous trifecta of combatting our emotions through repression, distraction or downright avoidance. We repress by pushing our feelings down, pretending they don't exist. We distract ourselves with work, hobbies or screen time to avoid dealing with uncomfortable emotions. Sometimes, we simply avoid situations that might trigger those feelings. And in more extreme cases, we completely numb our emotions through alcohol, drugs and other addictive substances. While these strategies might offer temporary relief, they often lead to greater emotional turmoil in the long run.

The re-emergence of stoic principles, although they certainly have some value in helping us live a good life, has contributed to this denial of our emotions. Many followers of stoicism preach that emotions are 'irrational' and should not be believed. Rather, we should live through morals, principles and logic alone. Despite stoicism being thousands of years old, modern self-help seems to be in the middle of a passionate love affair with its principles. Everywhere you turn online is another person preaching the importance of practising stoicism when it comes to emotional wellbeing. (I'm looking at you Mel Robbins, Ryan Holiday and Jordan Peterson.)

While merit can be found in maintaining composure and making rational decisions, dismissing emotions altogether can be harmful. Emotions are a fundamental part of the human experience; they provide valuable insights and can motivate you to take action in life. For instance, fear can signal danger, prompting you to take necessary precautions, while joy can reinforce behaviours that lead to positive outcomes. So instead of disregarding emotions, we should aim to understand them and to integrate them with rational thought to form a more balanced and whole perspective.

Toxic positivity has also led entire generations of people to mistakenly label emotions as either 'good' or 'bad'. Feelings such as 'motivated', 'loving' or 'happy' are deemed to be desirable or acceptable emotions, while feelings such as 'anxiety', 'overwhelm' and 'frustration' are categorised as unacceptable and bad. Unfortunately, though, you can't selectively pick and choose your emotions. When you try to numb your 'bad' emotions, you end up narrowing your entire emotional range. As shown in the following figure, you can end up feeling disconnected from all your emotions, even the 'good' ones. And maybe even more concerning, you can end up feeling disconnected from yourself.

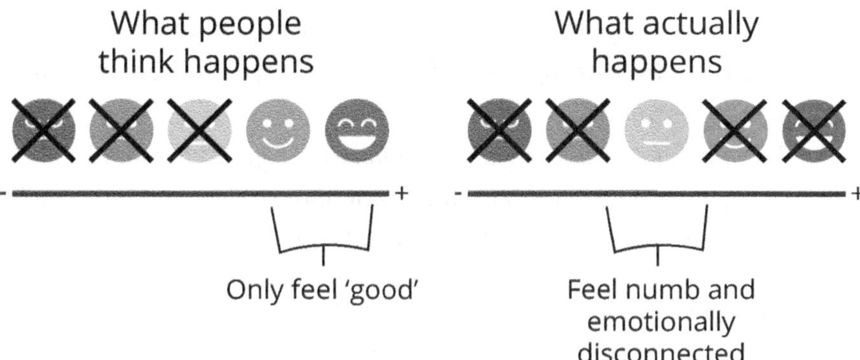

Trying to selectively numb your emotions

So if repression, avoidance, numbing, distraction, stoicism and toxic positivity aren't effective ways to navigate your emotions, what tools are left in the toolkit?

This is where our first happiness skill comes in: expanding your emotional intelligence. Perhaps this doesn't come as any sort of surprise. The gospel of emotional intelligence has been sung from the rafters since Daniel Goleman's groundbreaking book, *Emotional Intelligence: Why It Can Matter More Than IQ*, was published in 1995. Goleman's work highlighted how emotional intelligence (EQ) can be just as important, if not more so, than intellectual intelligence (IQ) in determining success and wellbeing.

In this chapter, I don't spend much time diving into the history of emotional intelligence. Instead, I outline three tools you can use to help you strengthen this skill. Through these three tools, you'll learn:

1. *What emotional intelligence actually is:* I run through the core components of emotional intelligence and how they manifest in everyday life.
2. *How to gauge your emotional intelligence levels:* I help you identify your strengths and areas for improvement through self-assessment.
3. *The most important steps to help maximise your emotional intelligence:* I provide key tools you can use to move towards emotional management and regulation.

By the end of this chapter, you'll have a clearer understanding of emotional intelligence and a set of my favourite tools and techniques to help you work with your emotions instead of fighting them all the time.

Understanding Goleman's five forms of emotional intelligence

As mentioned, Daniel Goleman introduced the world to the groundbreaking concept of emotional intelligence in 1995, highlighting just how crucial it could be both at work and in personal relationships. In his work, Goleman identified five key components of emotional intelligence:

1. self-awareness
2. self-regulation
3. motivation
4. empathy
5. social skills.

Before I explore how you can grow your emotional intelligence, I'm going to set the stage by touching briefly on each of these five components. As I do so, I encourage you to take a quiet moment of self-reflection and think about how well developed each component is in your personal skillset. You may find, for example, that you're quite strong at two of the five components, but that others would benefit from more attention, learning and practice.

Self-awareness

Self-awareness is the ability to recognise and understand your own emotions. It's like having an internal compass that guides your decisions and reactions.

Imagine Sarah, a project manager who always feels a knot in her stomach before presentations. Instead of ignoring this feeling, Sarah acknowledges her anxiety. She realises it's her body's way of signalling that public speaking is a challenge for her, and that it presents some risks. In this way, her anxiety is simply doing its job of trying to keep her safe from risks and threats.

With this insight, she can take steps to better manage her anxiety, such as practising her presentation or using deep-breathing exercises to calm herself. By acknowledging her emotions and facing them head-on, Sarah is more likely to still be able to give that important upcoming presentation at work.

Another good way to think of self-awareness is like you're holding up a mirror to your emotions. Just like a mirror provides perspective over your appearance, self-awareness helps you gain perspective and understanding over your emotional responses.

Self-regulation

Self-regulation is the ability to manage your emotions, especially under stress, and maintain control over your impulses. Where self-awareness gives you the ability to recognise and acknowledge your emotions, self-regulation gives you the ability to work with them in healthy ways. This is why it's crucial to develop self-awareness prior to building self-regulation skills. Put simply—you cannot hope to manage something if you can't see it in the first place.

Consider John, who receives critical feedback from his boss. His initial reaction is to get defensive. This makes sense—his 'fight-or-flight' response has been activated and, in this case, it's ready and raring to fight back. Instead of emotionally reacting, however, John pauses, takes a deep breath and processes his emotions. John acknowledges his frustration and understands that his brain is trying to protect him, but that in this case it may not be the healthiest response.

Instead, thanks to building his self-regulation skills, John chooses to respond calmly. He thanks his boss for the feedback and asks for specific ways to improve. He also clearly communicates his perspectives and calmly disagrees with some of the points his boss has made. This measured response not only defuses a potentially tense situation but also opens the door for constructive dialogue.

Self-regulation is like being the captain of a ship during a storm. Even when the waves are crashing, as the captain you ideally will be able to remain calm and steer your ship with a steady hand. Similarly, self-regulation allows you to navigate the usual emotional turbulence of life with composure, ensuring that you can be emotionally responsive rather than emotionally reactive.

Motivation

Of Goleman's five components of emotional intelligence, motivation is arguably the most known. In the realm of emotional intelligence, motivation refers to having the inner drive to pursue goals with energy and persistence. It's about finding joy in the process and striving for excellence.

Now, a key term is hidden in that description that's critical to highlight: 'inner drive'. We can often rely too much on external motivation (sometimes called 'extrinsic motivation') and under-emphasise inner drive (sometimes called 'intrinsic motivation') when it comes to pursuing our goals. External motivation is driven by external rewards such as money, fame, grades or praise. While it can be effective in the short term, it often leads to burnout and a lack of fulfilment. Internal motivation, on the other hand, is driven by internal rewards such as personal growth, passion and a sense of purpose. This type of motivation is more powerful and sustainable in the long run because it aligns with your core values and interests. I dive more deeply into this distinction over the coming chapters, but for now let's have a look at motivation in action.

Take Maria, a teacher who is deeply committed to her students' success. Despite the challenges of her job, she stays intrinsically motivated by focusing on the positive impact she has on her students' lives. Maria sets personal goals for professional development and continuously seeks new teaching methods to keep her students engaged and excited about learning. By remaining deeply connected to why she values teaching in the first place, Maria's sense of overall motivation remains higher than her colleagues who have disconnected from their inner drive.

Empathy

Now we move from the often over-emphasised and over-pursued component of emotional intelligence, motivation, to what is often the most overlooked and under-practiced component: empathy. Empathy is the ability to understand and share the feelings of others. It involves being sensitive to others' emotions and responding with compassion and support. When it comes to living a happy, fulfilling and flourishing life, empathy is certainly one of the most important skills to consistently hone.

Imagine Emily, a manager who notices one of her team members, James, has been unusually quiet and withdrawn. Instead of ignoring it, Emily takes the time to talk to James privately, expressing her concern and offering support. Through empathy, she learns that James is dealing with a personal issue. Emily's understanding and supportive response helps James feel valued and less isolated. In this example, Emily being attuned to James's emotions and behaviour not only helped him feel more supported but, according to numerous studies, also likely made Emily feel happier.

Of course, as with many skills and frameworks explored in this book, being empathetic is much easier said than done. But with consistent practice, reflection and refinement, empathy will eventually grant you a more finely tuned emotional radar. It can help you to pick up on the subtle emotional cues of others, and guide you towards healthier, happier and more humanistic responses. By being empathetic, you not only strengthen your own emotional intelligence but also support the emotional wellbeing and flourishing of those around you.

Social skills

Last, but certainly not least in Goleman's five components of emotional intelligence, is social skills. Social skills relate to your ability to build and maintain healthy relationships, communicate effectively and navigate social situations with ease. While empathy opens the door for enriching relationships and social interactions, social skills are what help you to walk through that door and cultivate meaningful connections with others.

Consider Tom, a team leader who excels at resolving conflicts and fostering a collaborative team environment. When a disagreement arises between team members, Tom uses his social skills to mediate the situation. He listens to both sides, encourages open communication and helps the team find a mutually beneficial solution. Tom's ability to manage relationships and communicate effectively makes him a respected and effective leader.

Social skills are the glue that holds a team together. Taking this a few steps further, I'd even say that when social skills are upheld by empathy, they form the glue that holds humankind together. They enable us to connect with each other, to healthily resolve conflict, to bridge divisions and to create more positive social environments. And we deeply need all these things as a global society.

Reflection and application

Take some time now to reflect on each of the five components of emotional intelligence and how they appear in your own life. Consider:

- Which components have you managed to strengthen through your years?

(continued)

- Which components do you recognise as being somewhat underdeveloped and would benefit from improvement?

Keeping an eye out for moments in life that give you a chance to practise one of the five components can be useful. Chances are, a lot of opportunities present themselves each day for you to sharpen your emotional intelligence.

Gauging your emotional intelligence levels in five stages

Goleman's five components form the perfect foundations from which to develop your emotional intelligence. But on their own they don't provide enough context as to what the journey of better managing your emotions actually looks like. This is where the next two models come in handy.

During the past eight years I've been fortunate enough to deliver over 10 000 personal happiness coaching sessions with people from all walks of life. While their situations, challenges and life history were unique to them as individuals, I began noticing a curious pattern when it came to their level of emotional intelligence. I named this pattern the 'five stages of emotional intelligence'—which, admittedly, is easy to confuse with Goleman's five components of emotional intelligence. Thankfully, as shown in the following figure, the two frameworks work quite nicely together, with the stages built on the foundations of Goleman's components.

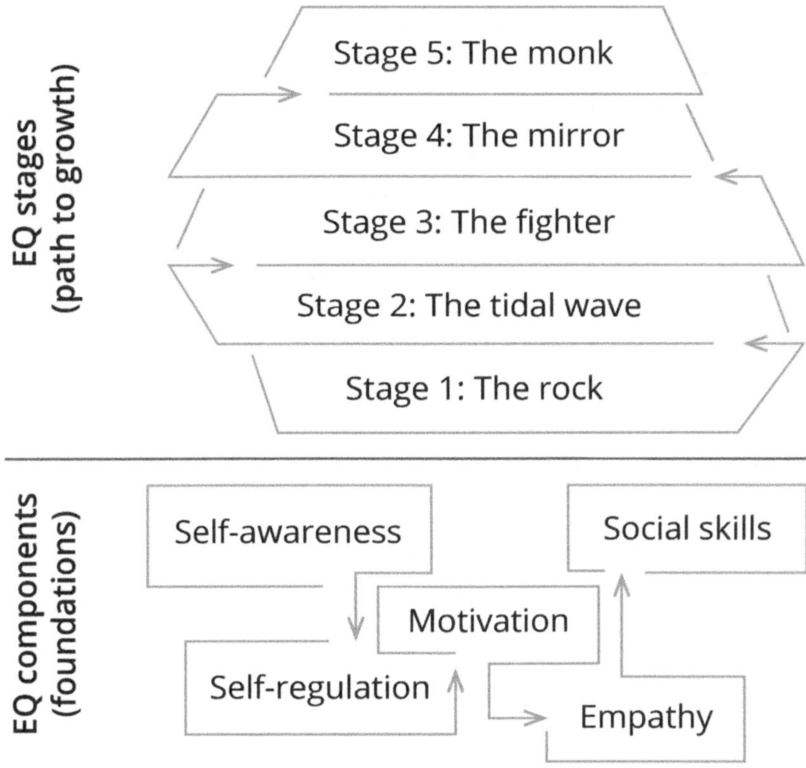

The five stages of emotional intelligence

Before I explore each stage in more depth, it's important to highlight that progressing up the stages is not like a game of *Super Mario.* That is to say, you don't progress to a higher level and then have a save point that prevents you from returning to lower levels. Everybody 'visits' and 'revisits' each stage, even if only for brief moments. And no matter how developed your emotional intelligence becomes, I promise you that you'll still have moments where you slip back to the lower levels.

The reason I'm sharing this is because I don't want you to set yourself the unrealistic expectation of always being highly emotionally intelligent. The goal isn't to reach stage five and stay there. The goal is to become more aware of the five stages and be able to move back up them when you slip back down. Ideally, you become able to progress up the stages more quickly than you did previously. But you will never 'perfect' your emotional intelligence.

As I run through each of the five distinct stages in more detail, reflect on how much time you generally spend in each stage. If you were to look at a usual day or week of your life, which of the five stages is your most dominant?

The rock: Emotionally unaware

The first stage is the 'rock'—and, no, I didn't name it after Dwayne 'the Rock' Johnson. I can't personally comment on his level of emotional intelligence, but it seems he may have reached some higher stages than this one. The reason I called stage one the 'rock' is because when we spend a lot of time in this stage, we become emotionally numb. We are disconnected from our emotions and even unaware of them. Our main emotional coping strategies at this stage are to repress our feelings, distract ourselves from them by keeping our mind busy, or numb them completely.

The issue with this approach is that no matter how much you try to ignore your emotions, they're still there bubbling away below the surface. And keeping them pushed down takes a whole lot of energy. Quite frankly, it's exhausting to repress your emotions for so much of your life.

This isn't to say that people who spend the majority of their time at stage one are at fault. At some stage in each of our lives, we have all spent a majority of our time avoiding, repressing, numbing or distracting ourselves from our feelings. If you were lucky enough to learn a little bit about emotional intelligence over the years—either from your parents, your schooling or from your own personal development—you've likely been able to move up a couple of stages.

But consider the people you know who were never really exposed to healthy emotional intelligence in their childhood. They didn't have emotionally intelligent parents modelling what it looks like to express emotion in healthy ways. They then didn't learn about these things at school. For their whole life, they may have actually been taught the opposite—through stereotyped sayings like 'boys don't cry', 'it's weak to show emotion', or even the seemingly innocent comment 'you shouldn't feel like that'. Over the months and years of their lives, these 'rules' have shaped how they approach their emotions, until eventually all they know how to do is disconnect from their emotions entirely.

Whenever someone tells me that 'they're just not an emotional person' or that they know someone in their life who 'doesn't really have emotions', it's often a sign that they're spending a lot of their life stuck in stage one. Sometimes I have conversations with people who share with me that they feel like they're 'just not good at emotions' or they 'suck at managing their emotions'. I often reply with the same question: 'When did you last intentionally practice managing your emotions in healthy ways?' They often reply with 'never' or 'not since I was a child'.

In a similar sentiment, I often used to find myself saying things like, 'I suck at art' or, 'I'm just not good at painting'. I'd see the amazing visual art skills some of my friends had and wish that I could paint and draw like they could. I remember one of these experiences in particular changed everything for me. I was admiring an artwork that a friend had created and in passing said, 'I could never do that. I'm terrible at drawing'.

My friend turned to me and very casually asked me, 'Well, when did you last intentionally practice drawing?' I stopped and thought for a moment before sheepishly admitting it hadn't been since I was around eight years old. Without missing a beat, my friend said, 'So are you terrible at drawing, or do you just draw with the skills of an eight year old?'

Now, when someone who is stuck at stage one says to me that they 'suck at managing their emotions', I share this story and ask, 'So, do you suck at managing your emotions? Or do you just manage your emotions with the skills of a child?'

Now, if you're reading this and thinking, *That might be me,* I want to highlight something important. It may not be your fault that you haven't yet developed your emotional intelligence past stage one, but it is now your responsibility to do so. Even in sharing that message, I know that I'm likely 'preaching to the choir'. Unfortunately, it's rare for someone who is stuck at stage one to be even reading a book like this. So perhaps a more valuable message to share is this: if you're reading this and thinking of someone in your life who you care about — someone who you can see is stuck at stage one — maybe it's worth gifting them a copy of this book. You can do so without the expectation that they will do anything with it and without any sense of judgement or obligation. You can simply offer it as an invitation and a sign of support, letting them know that you're there for them.

Because, at the end of the day, we all spend a bit of time in stage one. Even after doing this work for over a decade, I still have moments where I binge-watch Netflix to avoid an uncomfortable feeling. I still have moments when I use quick dopamine hits like sugary food or coffee to give me a short-term pep up and to distract myself temporarily from an emotion I don't want to deal with. I still have moments when I can't quite recognise or name an emotion I'm experiencing because I'm disconnected from it. The benefit of developing our emotional intelligence is we begin to be able to recognise when we're stuck in stage one and to grow through it faster than if we hadn't ever worked on these skills.

The tidal wave: Emotionally reactive

As you progress from stage one to stage two on the emotional intelligence scale, one of the first things you can be confronted with is how overwhelming your emotions are. At this stage, you become increasingly aware of your emotions because they're big, loud and at times all-consuming. It's as though, having been ignored while you were in stage one, your emotions are now shouting at you at full volume to get your attention.

This is why I call stage two the 'tidal wave'—because you're now feeling your emotions, but they're coming at you like a tidal wave. This stage is often experienced in childhood, but that doesn't exclude adults from getting stuck in it. I know I can put my hand up and say I've had plenty of times in my life, and continue to have times, when I have felt completely overwhelmed by a feeling that seems to have snuck up out of nowhere and blindsided me. Whether it be sadness, worry, frustration, stress, or even a feeling like joy, love and gratitude, these feelings have often been bubbling away under the surface for a while and they've finally hit a threshold where they've broken through and got my full attention.

It's important to highlight that not all stage two experiences are difficult, or based on the emotions often labelled as 'challenging'.

You are equally as capable of being caught in a moment of overwhelming anxiety as you are of being caught in a moment of overwhelming joy. You can feel all-consuming stress as equally as you can feel 'head over heels', all-consuming love. Later in this chapter, I discuss the different approaches available in your emotional intelligence toolkit, based on whether you want to sustain a moment of emotional overwhelm or healthily navigate through it.

For now, though, simply remember that a very common, normal and completely understandable reaction to emotional overwhelm is to regress to stage one. Having been hit by the tidal wave of emotion you may, either consciously or subconsciously, begin to repress, avoid or distract yourself from your emotions once again. If you do this enough times—due, perhaps, to something blocking your progress through the five stages—it creates an exhausting cycle of prolonged periods of emotional disconnection followed by acute experiences of emotional overwhelm.

If, however, you choose not to avoid or bury these big emotions, and instead embrace emotional courage and elect to confront your feelings head on, you progress to stage three of the emotional intelligence scale.

The fighter: Emotionally resistant

As you move to stage three, you've chosen to face your feelings head-on rather than avoid them, repress them, bury them, distract yourself from them, or be completely overwhelmed and consumed by them. You're in the ring.

At this stage, you are often able to recognise and name the emotion you're experiencing, and may also be able to understand at least part of what has led to it. For example, you may be able to say, 'I'm feeling anxious because I have a lot of projects due at work at the same time and I feel as though I'm running out of time to complete them to my best ability. I'm worried that I'll end up letting people down and I'll make mistakes'.

This is a fantastic step forward from the first two stages of emotional intelligence. Unfortunately, one single factor can easily trip you up and either keep you stuck in stage three or even send you tumbling back to stage one. And that factor is judgement.

In stage three, we often label a wide range of emotions as 'difficult', 'challenging' or 'negative'. We judge the emotions and we judge ourselves for having them. We see these emotions not as messengers trying to communicate something to us, but as our opponents in the boxing ring. So we put the gloves on and prepare to fight the feelings. We use all the techniques we've picked up throughout life to 'beat' anxiety, we use all the tools we know to 'overcome' anger and we practice all the strategies we've even been taught about 'reducing' stress. And we do this all because of one foundational judgement: 'I shouldn't be feeling this way'.

This is why I call stage three 'the fighter'. And let me promise you something: I've never seen anyone consistently 'win' when they're fighting their own feelings. At best, they'll shift them momentarily and hold them at bay. At worst, they'll get stuck in a spiral of emotional resistance and self-judgement.

Consider this: have you ever felt frustrated at yourself for feeling nervous? Have you ever felt annoyed at your own feelings of sadness? While you may start with one feeling—let's say a feeling of anxiousness—your own emotional judgement and resistance can then cause a rapidly growing snowball of feelings, as shown in the following figure (overleaf).

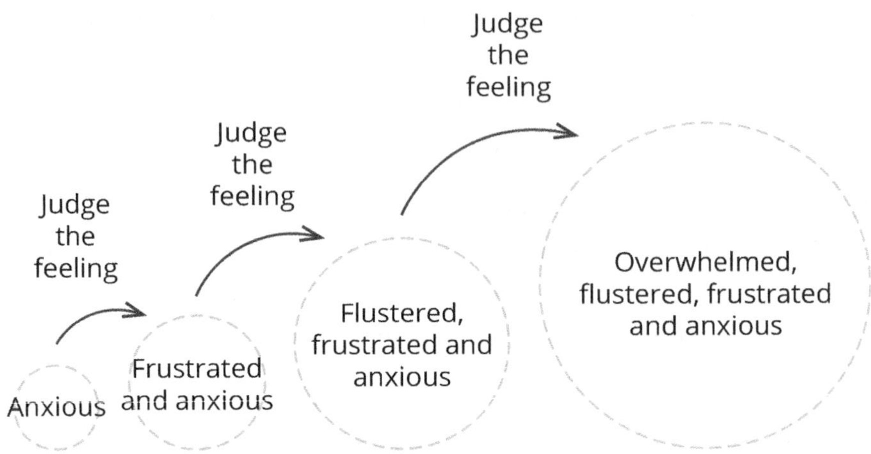

The emotional snowball effect

Eventually, the snowball gets so big, or the boxing match you're in with your own feelings goes on for so long, that you become completely and utterly exhausted. Before long, you don't have the capacity to do anything except, you guessed it, return to stage one by repressing, avoiding or distracting yourself from your emotions.

This cycle through the first three stages of the emotional intelligence scale is the most common pattern I see—and for good reason. A huge chasm separates stage three and stage four, along with potential blockers. To cross this gap and overcome your own blockers, you need a couple of distinct emotional intelligence tools at your disposal. Unless you've intentionally worked on your personal development or invested in learning about emotional intelligence, you may have never come across the specific tools required to progress to the higher levels of stages four and five.

Before I unpack the tools required to unlock these higher stages of emotional intelligence, let's figure out what they actually look and feel like.

The mirror: Emotionally reflective

Stage four is where real change begins. It's the point at which you start recognising your emotional patterns, identifying how your thoughts and feelings impact your decisions, and reflecting on the way you show up in different situations. But, as the name suggests, this awareness often comes *after* the fact—like looking in the rear-view mirror once the road rage has already taken over, or realising hours later that you snapped at a loved one because you were stressed about work.

At this stage, emotions still hijack the driver's seat. They take control in the moment, and you only regain your awareness once the emotional storm has settled. This is the difference between reacting and responding—at this stage, you are still reacting, but you're learning to reflect, adjust and course-correct after the fact.

Think about a time when you were exhausted after a long day. Perhaps someone asked you a simple question, but you responded with irritation or impatience. In the moment, you didn't pause to consider why you felt irritable; your emotions simply took over. But later that night, as you replayed the situation in your mind, you realised your frustration wasn't really about that person; it was about your own exhaustion. Maybe you even thought, *Next time, I'll take a deep breath before responding.*

This is the essence of the mirror stage: learning from your emotional responses so you can do better next time. This process—pausing to analyse how you felt, what triggered you and what you might do differently in the future—builds the foundation for higher emotional intelligence. Neuroscience supports this idea, showing that self-reflection strengthens the prefrontal cortex, the part of our brains responsible for emotional regulation and decision-making.

At this level, curiosity is key. Rather than judging yourself harshly for how you reacted, approach your emotions with openness. Ask yourself, 'Why did I respond that way?', 'What was I feeling in that moment?' and 'What can I learn from this experience?' This kind of introspection helps rewire your brain, creating new neural pathways that make emotional regulation easier over time.

It's important to note that stage four is still reactive. The goal here isn't to be perfect, but to notice, reflect and begin making small adjustments. Every time you take a moment to step back and learn from your emotions, you are building the muscle of emotional intelligence. And you're stepping closer to the next stage—where interacting with your thoughts and feelings doesn't just happen after the fact, but in the moment

The monk: Emotionally responsive

At the fifth stage, which I call the 'monk', the game changes. Instead of emotions taking the wheel and you reflecting later, you learn to catch them *before* they dictate your actions. You become proactive rather than reactive. You recognise your emotions in real-time and make conscious decisions about how you respond to them.

This doesn't mean suppressing emotions or pretending they don't exist—quite the opposite. It means acknowledging them, understanding their message and choosing your response with intention. Imagine you're driving a metaphorical bus of emotions but, instead of letting anxiety or anger take the wheel, you're in control. The emotions are still there, offering their input from the passenger seats, but you decide which direction to take.

For example, let's say you feel irritation rising during a tense conversation. Instead of immediately snapping or shutting down, you notice the feeling as it arises. You take a breath. You remind yourself, *This frustration is valid, but it doesn't have to dictate my response.* You choose to communicate assertively instead of aggressively. In that moment, you've just practised emotional intelligence at the monk level.

Research from the Greater Good Science Center at UC Berkeley highlights that mindfulness—the ability to observe emotions without being controlled by them—leads to greater emotional regulation, reduced stress and increased wellbeing. This is the essence of the monk stage: emotions still influence you, but they no longer control you.

Getting to this stage requires patience, practice and a willingness to fail. It won't happen overnight. You'll have moments when old habits creep in and emotions take over before you can stop them. But every time you catch yourself sooner than you did before, you're making progress.

The feeling most often associated with this stage is a sense of calm confidence—an inner knowing that no matter what emotions arise, you have the tools to handle them. You are no longer at their mercy. Instead, you can harness them, allowing them to guide you without dictating your behaviour.

This ability to experience emotions fully while still making choices that align with your values is what emotional mastery looks like. You have the ability to feel deeply without being consumed and to steer your own ship, no matter how stormy the waters.

As shown in the following figure, this is the ultimate goal of emotional intelligence. You're not aiming to become emotionless, but to become emotionally free—fully engaged in life, yet fully in the driver's seat of your decisions and behaviours.

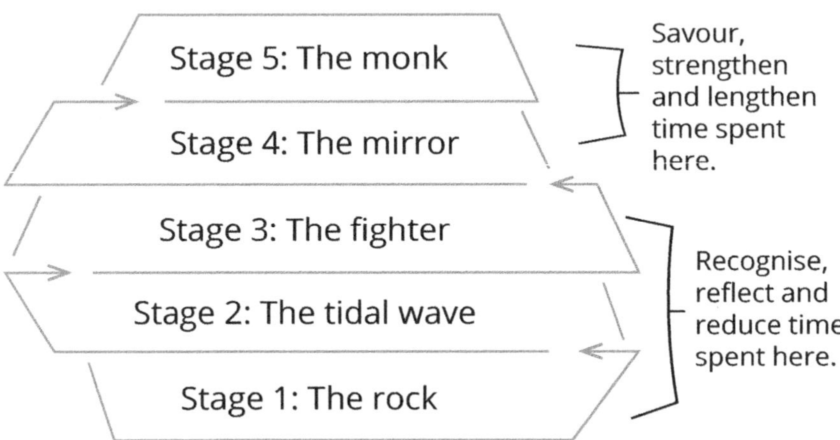

The goal of healthy emotional intelligence

If there's one thing I want to recommunicate, make abundantly clear and remind you of as I wrap up this section, it's this: the goal is not to reach stage five and stay there forever. That's not how emotional intelligence works, and it's certainly not how being human works. Even after over a decade of studying happiness and emotional intelligence, I still experience moments of stage one (ignorance is bliss), stage two (the sucky bit), and every other stage after—sometimes all in the same day.

Emotional intelligence isn't a mountain you climb once and then plant your flag at the top. It's more like a dance, where you're constantly moving between stages depending on the situation, your energy levels, your stress load and even the people around you. Some days, you might operate mostly at stage four or five, catching your emotions early and responding with wisdom. Other days, you might slip down to stage three, where emotions take over momentarily and you only recognise it after the fact. That's normal. That's human.

So the goal isn't to be perfect at emotional intelligence, but to *practise* your emotional intelligence. You're aiming to develop the ability to quickly recognise which stage you're in, and then have the skills, tools and self-compassion to work your way back up when needed. Emotional intelligence isn't about never being overwhelmed, never snapping at someone or never making a rash decision. It's about catching yourself sooner when those things happen and course-correcting with intention.

And that's exactly what we're going to focus on next. Now that you understand the five stages of emotional intelligence, in the next section I explore the tools and techniques that will help you move up the scale more effectively. These are the practices that will help you build resilience, manage emotions in real time and, ultimately, show up as the best version of yourself more often than not.

Reflection and application

Before you move on, take a moment to notice how the five-stage model shows up in your life. You don't need to make any changes yet. You're just focusing on curiosity-led awareness. Ask yourself:

- How do you avoid or numb your emotions (stage one response)? What's your go-to? Examples include repressing, distracting (doom-scrolling, snacking, 'busywork'), over-intellectualising, joking it away, people-pleasing, overworking and alcohol.

(continued)

- Which feelings do you most often wrestle with (stage three response)? Anger? Anxiety? Shame? Frustration?
- How can you intentionally seek out and savour moments when you're in stage four (the mirror) or stage five (the monk)? This is when you notice, name and allow a feeling, and when you sit with calm, clear presence and choose a values-aligned response.

Building emotional intelligence with five key tools

If you cast your mind back to stage one (the 'rock'), you'll remember that the biggest thing keeping you stuck there is avoidance. At this stage, you're repressing, numbing, disconnecting—basically doing whatever you can to not face what you're feeling. Emotions are pushed aside rather than acknowledged and, as a result, you end up feeling lost, confused or stuck in a cycle of unhealthy coping mechanisms.

So, if avoidance is what traps us at stage one, the way forward is clear: we need to start practising emotional awareness and expanding our emotional literacy.

Making the leap from stage one to stage two: Learning to surf the emotional waves

You've probably heard the saying, 'What we feel, we can heal'. But before you can even feel something properly, you first need to name it. Sensing that something is wrong emotionally but not having the words to describe it can be incredibly daunting. It's unsettling.

It creates a feeling of being out of control, like trying to navigate without a map. But when you have the vocabulary to accurately label what you're feeling, you regain a sense of clarity and control.

Put simply, if you want to tame your emotions, you must first name them.

Why emotional literacy matters

Some solid science exists behind this idea of emotional literacy. A study conducted by UCLA psychologist Matthew Lieberman found that putting feelings into words actually reduces their intensity. Brain scans showed that when people labelled their emotions, activity in the amygdala (the part of the brain responsible for processing emotions) decreased, while activity in the prefrontal cortex (responsible for rational thought) increased. Essentially, naming emotions helps us regulate them.

Despite this, many of us are terrible at accurately identifying our emotions. If you asked the average person how they're feeling, you'd likely hear one of five responses: good, bad, not bad, alright or getting there. Note that none of these are actual emotions.

In fact, many highly developed countries—including Australia, New Zealand, the United Kingdom, Canada and the United States—have a significant emotional literacy gap. We are taught maths, science and grammar in school, yet many of us are never explicitly taught how to recognise, label or express our emotions beyond the basics of happy, sad or angry.

This is where the Feelings Wheel (which I introduced in chapter 1) comes back into play. I previously used the Feelings Wheel to explore how happiness is an umbrella term that includes a whole range of distinct emotions. Now, I want you to zoom out and consider the entire wheel.

The gold standard for emotional literacy is being able to recognise and name at least 30 distinct feelings. That means when someone asks how you're feeling, you're not just saying 'fine' or 'stressed', but instead have the vocabulary to say:

- 'I feel a sense of awe and inspiration.'
- 'I feel overstimulated and restless.'
- 'I feel disappointed and let down.'

But let's be real—most people aren't anywhere near being able to name 30 feelings. So where do we start?

The two-word check-in

One of the most effective ways to build emotional awareness is a simple technique I call the 'two-word check-in'. Here's how it works: at random points during your day, pause and ask yourself, 'If I had to describe how I'm feeling right now in just two words, what would they be?'

Why does this work? Because it forces you to cut through the head noise and get straight to the emotion. Too often, when we're asked how we're feeling, we don't actually name feelings at all—we name context or thoughts instead. For example, if you ask someone how they're feeling, they might say, 'Work's been really busy lately, and I've got this major project due, and my boss keeps checking in on me'. That's context, not emotion.

If you press further, they might say, 'I'm worried that if I don't meet the deadline, I'll let my boss down, and then I won't be put on any more big projects'. That's thoughts, not emotion.

But when you do a two-word check-in, you bypass all of that and get straight to the core. In this case, the person might finally say, 'I feel anxious and inferior'.

Now we're getting somewhere. Once you can name the emotions, you can work with them. Instead of becoming consumed by a tidal wave of emotions (stage two), you improve your ability to surf the emotional waves of life.

Reflection and application

Over the next 30 days, commit to these simple but powerful exercises to start bridging the gap between emotional avoidance and emotional awareness:

1. **Daily Feelings Wheel review:**
   - Print out a Feelings Wheel (or save one to your phone).
   - Spend a few minutes each day looking at it.
   - Over time, challenge yourself to tick off at least 30 emotions that you confidently recognise and understand.
2. **The two-word check-in:**
   - Set two to three random reminders on your phone each day.
   - When the reminder goes off, pause and identify your emotions in two words. No over-explaining, no justifying — just two words.
3. **Emotion journaling:**
   - Each night, write down three emotions you experienced during the day and what triggered them.
   - Reflect on whether they were helpful or unhelpful, and how you responded.

By consistently applying these reflection and application tools, you'll begin to bridge the gap from emotional avoidance to emotional awareness. You'll start noticing emotions sooner and identifying them more accurately. Most importantly, you'll be taking the first step towards greater emotional intelligence.

Because the truth is emotions aren't something to fear or repress. They're signals, messengers and teachers. And the more fluent you become in understanding them, the more empowered you'll be in shaping your life and becoming happier.

Progressing from stage two to stage three: Putting down the gloves

By now, you've started recognising your emotions more clearly. You've moved past the fog of emotional avoidance and are beginning to name what you're feeling with more precision. What you've also likely found out quite quickly is that the simple act of naming your feelings reduces the intensity a little. They no longer feel like a tidal wave of emotions that will engulf and drown you. Now, don't get me wrong, the wave can still feel big and daunting. But it's definitely more manageable. This is when you can start learning to surf the emotional waves of life rather than fighting them.

Previously at stage two, emotions felt intrusive, uncomfortable and even overwhelming. Understandably, your instinct was likely to wrestle with them—to push them away, suppress them or intellectualise them until they 'make sense'. But here's the uncomfortable truth: this is not a fight you're going to win.

No-one has ever conquered sadness by arguing with it. No-one has ever permanently evicted anxiety from their mind. The more you resist emotions, the stronger they fight back. It's like trying to force an uninvited guest out of a party—they'll dig their heels in, make a bigger scene and refuse to leave until they've been properly acknowledged.

So what do you do instead? You put down the gloves and accept what is already here.

What emotional acceptance really means (and what it doesn't)

Let's be clear: accepting your emotions does not mean agreeing with them. It doesn't mean you like what you're feeling. It doesn't mean you're throwing your hands up in defeat or resigning yourself to a life of discomfort. It simply means acknowledging that the feeling is here, in this moment, whether you want it to be or not.

Russ Harris, one of the leading researchers in acceptance and commitment therapy (ACT), puts it simply: 'Struggling with emotions is like struggling in quicksand—the more you fight, the deeper you sink'. The way out isn't through force, but through allowing.

Returning to our metaphorical bus, all emotions are passengers on the bus of your mind. Some, like excitement and confidence, are enjoyable company. Others, like fear and frustration, make for more difficult travel companions. But none of them can be kicked off the bus—at least, not permanently. The goal isn't to banish uncomfortable emotions; it's to let them take a seat, acknowledge them, and continue driving in the direction you want to go.

And when we stop fighting our emotions, something remarkable happens—they start revealing their deeper messages. Take anger, for example. It's a strong, often overwhelming feeling that can lead to reactive behaviours. But what happens when you sit with it instead of acting on it? What happens when you get curious instead of combative?

Perhaps you've heard the following popular quote (often misattributed to CS Lewis): 'I sat with my anger long enough until she told me her real name was grief'. Despite its unclear origins, this captures this sentiment perfectly, highlighting that anger wasn't the root feeling; it was the bodyguard. Underneath it was something more vulnerable, and something that needed attention. If you had fought the anger during this time, you would have been wrestling with the symptom, not the underlying root cause.

This is why stage three isn't just about awareness. It's also about becoming an emotional explorer. Instead of seeing emotions as threats to be eliminated, you start listening to what they have to say.

Now, before you go pulling up a chair and hosting deep conversations with every fleeting emotion, it's important to find balance. Yes, you want to acknowledge and accept your feelings, but you don't want to stew in them forever.

Studies show that excessive rumination, the act of repeatedly dwelling on emotions without resolution, can actually exacerbate anxiety and depression. Overthinking an emotion doesn't actually help you process it. Instead, it traps you in it.

Here's how to understand the difference between healthy emotional reflection and rumination:

- Healthy reflection is about noticing and naming emotions, and then deciding what to do with them.
- Rumination is about looping the same thoughts without progress, replaying scenarios without resolution, or getting stuck in 'why me?' thinking.

A great in-the-moment tool to avoid rumination is to add a simple phrase to your two-word check-in: 'I am feeling flustered and scattered ... right now, and that's okay'.

That little addition—'right now, and that's okay'—does two powerful things:

1. *It reminds you that emotions are temporary.* No feeling lasts forever, even if it feels like it in the moment.
2. *It removes the need for immediate action.* You don't have to fix or change what you're feeling. You just have to allow it to be there.

When you can do this consistently, something shifts. Stage three is no longer about being the fighter. Instead, you step into the role of the explorer.

Explorers don't panic when they encounter rough terrain. They don't curse the mountain for being steep or the river for being cold. They adapt, observe and keep moving forward.

And that's exactly what emotional intelligence at stage three is all about—seeing emotions for what they are, understanding their role, and moving forward with them rather than against them.

Reflection and application

Over the next 30 days, practise these steps to build emotional acceptance:

1. **Acknowledge, don't argue:**
   - When you experience a strong emotion, pause and say to yourself, 'This feeling is here right now, and that's okay'.
   - Remember you don't need to fix it; just notice it.

(continued)

2. **Check for the root emotion:**
   - When a difficult emotion arises, ask yourself, 'Is this the primary emotion, or is it covering up something deeper?'
   - If you feel anger, for example, is it protecting sadness? If you feel frustration, is it covering fear?
3. **Set a timer for reflection:**
   - If you tend to overanalyse, give yourself five to ten minutes to reflect on an emotion, and then move forward.
   - Journaling can help — write it down, set the timer, and then close the book and shift your focus.

By applying these practices, you'll start moving out of emotional resistance and into emotional acceptance. You'll learn to sit with emotions rather than suppress them, listen instead of fight and, ultimately, start navigating your emotions with more clarity, confidence and control. Welcome to your new and improved stage three: the 'emotional explorer'—where emotions become guides, not enemies.

Emotionally exploring your way from stage three to stage four: Recognising patterns

A certain moment comes in every explorer's journey when they stop looking at the map and start understanding the terrain. At stage three, you became aware of your emotions—you gave them names, stopped running from them and let them sit beside you without immediately reacting. But stage four (the mirror) is where you start recognising the deeper patterns beneath them. It's where you stop just experiencing emotions and start understanding them.

Because here's the thing—emotions aren't random. They don't just appear out of nowhere, and they certainly don't exist in isolation. Every emotion you feel has a story, a physical signature and a purpose. The problem is most of us have never been taught to read them properly.

So let's start reading between the lines of your emotions.

You are not your emotions (but they are trying to tell you something)

It's funny how often we let emotions define us. We say, 'I am anxious', 'I am angry' or 'I am sad'. But think about it—would you say, 'I am a headache' or 'I am hunger'? No, because you recognise those as experiences, not as part of your identity. Emotions work the same way. Just because you feel anger, sadness or anxiety doesn't mean that's who you are. And just because an emotion feels real doesn't mean it's factual.

We tend to treat emotions as absolute truth—'I feel it, so it must be real'. But emotions aren't reality. They are our brain's best guess about what's happening, based on past experiences, beliefs and subconscious patterns. For example, if you've been rejected before, your brain might tell you 'people don't value me' when a friend forgets to reply to your message. If you've grown up associating rest with laziness, you might feel guilty whenever you take a break. Your emotions are like a loyal but sometimes misinformed friend. They mean well, but they don't always get the full picture.

Instead of accepting every emotion as truth, get curious about them. Ask:

- 'What is this emotion trying to tell me?'
- 'Is this feeling based on fact, or is it based on an old story I've been telling myself?'
- 'If I viewed this emotion as a signal rather than a reality, how would that change my response?'

Mind cues: The thoughts that shape your emotions

Emotions don't just appear in isolation but come with a whole mental soundtrack. The problem is we rarely notice it playing in the background. For example:

- *Anxiety often brings thoughts of uncertainty and worst-case scenarios:* 'What if I fail?' 'What if they think I'm not good enough?'
- *Anger is fuelled by thoughts of blame or injustice:* 'This isn't fair.' 'They did this on purpose.'
- *Guilt whispers self-criticism:* 'I should have done better.' 'I'm letting people down.'

But here's where it gets interesting—two people can feel the same emotion for completely different reasons. Imagine two people are both feeling anxious before a big presentation. One might be anxious because they're afraid of messing up. The other might be anxious because they desperately want to impress people. They're feeling the same emotion, but with a different soundtrack.

This is why self-awareness matters. If you don't examine the stories your emotions are telling you, they'll keep dictating your reactions without you even realising it.

So next time you feel a strong emotion, pause for a moment. Instead of just saying, 'I feel anxious', try asking, 'What thoughts are coming up with this emotion?' You might start noticing patterns you never saw before.

Body cues: The physical language of emotion

Emotions live not just in your mind but also in your body. When you feel something, your body responds before you even realise it. Research backs this up, finding that physiological responses to emotions are largely automatic and universal. For example:

- Anxiety often shows up as a racing heart, shallow breathing or a tight chest.
- Anger can make your face feel hot, your jaw clench and your movements more forceful.
- Sadness might feel like heavy limbs, slower breathing or tightness in your throat.

Interestingly, some emotions feel almost identical in the body. Take nervousness and excitement, for example. Both cause increased heart rate, butterflies in the stomach and heightened energy. The key difference is your brain's interpretation:

- If your brain views the situation as a threat, you feel nervous.
- If your brain views it as a positive challenge, you feel excited.

This means you can train yourself to reframe certain emotions by simply recognising how they show up in your body.

The next time you feel a strong emotion, instead of overthinking it, tune into your body. Ask yourself:

- 'Where do I feel this emotion physically?'
- 'If I had to describe this sensation to a five year old, what would I say?'

Instead of saying, 'I feel stressed', you might describe it as, 'It feels like my chest is tight, my shoulders are tense and my breathing is shallow'.

Getting specific about how emotions feel in your body helps you process them faster—because once you recognise the pattern, you can start working with it rather than against it.

Reflection and application

Now that you're recognising the unique patterns of emotions in your mind and body, it's time to take this a step further.

Think of this like creating your own personal emotional recipe cards — giving you a guide to how emotions show up for you, so you can start recognising patterns before they take over.

Try this:

1. Pick an emotion — for example, stress, joy, sadness, frustration or excitement. Pick whatever feels relevant.
2. Break this emotion down into three levels:
   - Mild (low intensity)
   - Moderate (medium intensity)
   - Intense (high intensity)
3. For each level, write down:
   - *Mind cues:* What thoughts and beliefs show up?
   - *Body cues*: Where do you feel it physically?
   - *Trigger patterns:* What situations typically bring it up?

For example, for the emotion 'stress', you might write down the following:

- Mild stress:
  - *Mind cues:* 'I have a lot to do, but I can handle it.'
  - *Body cues:* Slight tension in shoulders, faster breathing.
- Moderate stress:
  - *Mind cues:* 'I'm starting to fall behind.'
  - *Body cues:* Jaw tightening, restlessness, fidgeting.
- Intense stress:
  - *Mind cues:* 'I can't do this, I'm completely overwhelmed.'
  - *Body cues:* Racing heart, nausea, trouble focusing.

You can write your observations up as shown in the following figure to create your own emotional recipe cards.

Name the feeling: ____________________

	Mild	Moderate	Intense
What happens in your mind (psychological cues)			
What happens in your body (physiological cues)			
Situational triggers			

Emotional recipe card

The more you get to know your emotions like this, the less control they have over you.

Remember that stage four isn't about controlling emotions—it's about understanding them so well that they no longer control you. Once you start recognising these patterns in real-time, you'll naturally begin shifting from reactive to reflective. And that's when emotional intelligence really starts working for you.

Bridging the gap between stage four and stage five: Emotional management and regulation

By now, you've built a solid foundation. You're no longer blindly reacting to your emotions but are instead seeing them clearly, understanding their patterns, and recognising how they show up in your mind and body. That alone puts you miles ahead of most people.

But understanding emotions and working with them intentionally are two very different things.

This next stage is where you move from awareness to action. You're not just recognising emotions as they come and go; you're learning how to navigate, influence and even cultivate them. Most importantly, this stage is about developing the tools to regulate your emotions in a way that supports your wellbeing, your relationships and your ability to thrive in life.

Again, this isn't about controlling emotions or trying to suppress them. It's about knowing when to shift your emotional state and when to fully experience and process it. And to do that, we're going to explore two essential tools:

1. *Leveraging your emotions:* Knowing when to actively shift your emotional state.

2. *Leaning into your emotions:* Recognising when to fully experience them instead of resisting.

You've probably noticed that, sometimes, a shift in mood can happen instantly. You wake up grumpy, but then you get a text from a friend that makes you smile and suddenly the day doesn't seem so bad. Or maybe you're feeling sluggish, but you put on your favourite playlist and start moving, and within minutes you feel energised. This is emotional leveraging in action.

At its core, emotional leveraging is about understanding that emotions don't just happen. Instead, they are created by a combination of what's happening in your mind and your body.

Think of this as being a little like cooking. The flavour of your emotions is determined by the ingredients you put in:

- Your thoughts and beliefs are one set of ingredients.
- Your physical state and actions are another.

For example, imagine you're feeling unmotivated and sluggish. You can shift this both psychologically and physiologically:

- *Psychological shift:* Instead of thinking, *I just can't be bothered today*, try *What's one small step I can take?* or *How will I feel once I get started?*
- *Physiological shift:* Change your body state—stand up, stretch, get some fresh air or drink a glass of water.

It's crucial to highlight that if you want to really make a meaningful change to your emotions, you need to make a shift to both your psychological cues and your physiological cues. If you only change one of these things, your mood might shift for a few moments. But without both a mental and physical reset, your emotions will usually pull you back in. Like in a game of tug of war, whichever side has two elements on it will eventually win over the side that has only one. If your body is sending you cues of anxiousness and you're already feeling anxious, telling yourself calming affirmations might provide some temporary relief, but eventually your mind will lose the game of tug of war to the feeling of anxiousness and to the physiological cues that uphold it.

Emotional leveraging works best when emotions are mild or moderate—that is, when they're present but still manageable. If left unchecked, emotions like stress, frustration or self-doubt can spiral into something much harder to regulate.

Emotional leaning in: The only way out is through

What about when emotions aren't mild or moderate? What about those moments when you feel completely flooded—when anxiety grips your chest, sadness pulls you under or anger courses through your veins? At these times, emotional leveraging doesn't work.

When an emotion reaches its peak, trying to fight it is like trying to hold back a tidal wave with your bare hands. Good luck. Instead, sometimes the healthiest thing you can do is lean in.

Perhaps you remember (or have read to your children) the classic 1989 book *We're Going on a Bear Hunt* by Michael Rosen and Helen Oxenbury. If so, you likely know the line, 'We can't go over it. We can't go under it. Oh no! We've got to go through it!'

This is exactly how intense emotions work. You can't sidestep them. You can't ignore them away. You have to really experience them in order to move through them.

That means:

- *If you need to cry, don't just cry:* Have the best, most cathartic, snot-dripping-from-your-nose cry of your life.
- *If you're feeling frustrated, channel it:* Move your body, listen to music that matches your mood, write out everything that's irritating you.
- *If you're bored, lean into it:* Stare at the ceiling, embrace the nothingness, let yourself get so incredibly bored that you actually become bored of being bored.

Here's an important distinction, however: leaning in doesn't mean wallowing. To keep yourself from getting stuck in an emotional spiral, try the following:

1. *Set a timer:* Give yourself 15 to 30 minutes to fully feel the emotion, without judgement.
2. *Drop the resistance:* If you're sad, be sad. If you're bored, be bored. Commit to the emotion fully.
3. *Notice what happens:* Most emotions, when fully experienced, start to subside on their own.

The key here is to express emotions in a way that is healthy and doesn't harm anyone else. Your emotions are your responsibility to work with, not somebody else's. In saying this, you don't have to do it alone. Another way to make leaning in feel safer is to do it with a support system.

Having a safe space to be emotionally vulnerable and process your emotions out loud without fear of judgement is invaluable for emotional regulation and emotional intelligence. This could mean:

- opening up to a trusted friend, partner or family member who can simply hold space for you

- seeking out a professional such as a counsellor, therapist, psychologist or coach who is trained to guide you through difficult emotions
- joining a support group or community where emotional expression is welcomed and encouraged.

So many of us were taught to 'handle our emotions on our own', as if struggling in silence is a sign of strength. But research has shown that social support plays a significant role in emotional regulation. We regulate emotions far better in connection than in isolation. Sometimes, just knowing that someone is willing to sit with you in your emotions, without rushing you through them, can make all the difference. Whether through a deep conversation, a hug that lasts a little longer than usual or simply someone saying, 'I get it and I'm here', having support can make the process of leaning in feel a little less daunting.

And here's the best part: when you allow yourself to be vulnerable with the right people, you're not just benefiting yourself but also showing them that it's okay for them to do the same. You create a ripple effect of emotional intelligence.

Once you've leant into the emotion enough, you'll find that it naturally reduces to a mild or moderate level. And that's when you can shift into emotional leveraging, changing the cues that your mind and body give to your emotional state.

The art of savouring: Making enjoyable feelings last longer

Leaning in isn't only a valuable practice when confronted by intense levels of unhelpful or uncomfortable feelings. It's also incredibly useful for strengthening, lengthening and savouring your more enjoyable emotions.

There's something deeply ironic about the way we often treat emotions. We usually marinate in the difficult ones—obsessing over stress, frustration or disappointment. But when we feel proud, grateful or connected, we often rush through it like it's nothing.

Why? Our brains have a built-in bias toward noticing threats and problems more than positive experiences. This bias kept our ancestors alive, but in modern life it often makes us gloss over the good stuff. This is where savouring comes in. It's the art of leaning into enjoyable experiences and moments when you feel good.

Positive psychology research has found that people who actively savour and extend enjoyable emotions experience greater life satisfaction.

Take this as your invitation to linger in the good moments through the following:

- If you feel a sense of connection, pause and soak it in.
- If you feel proud of yourself, let that feeling stay a little longer.
- If you're laughing with a friend, be fully present in that moment.

Instead of rushing through joy, gratitude, love and pride, stretch those moments out. Let them last.

Reflection and application

Try this over the next week:

- *Catch yourself in a mild or moderate emotion and use emotional leveraging:* Shift one thought pattern and one body cue.

(continued)

- *When you feel an intense emotion, set a timer and lean in:* See what happens when you stop resisting and just let yourself feel.
- *Practise savouring:* Next time you feel joy, love or pride, pause. Let it stay a little longer.

Continuing your practice: Emotional integration

As we near the end of this chapter on emotional intelligence, my hope is that you've gathered something powerful, and have a deeper understanding of your emotions and how to work with them. We've explored the five stages of emotional intelligence, recognised the patterns of your feelings and learned strategies to navigate them more effectively. Hopefully, you've even had a few 'aha moments' along the way.

But understanding something in theory and actually living it are two very different things. Knowing how to swim, for example, is different from jumping into the deep end of the pool. Reading about emotional intelligence is one thing. Applying it, especially in the heat of the moment, is another.

This is where embodied wisdom comes in. You're not just collecting knowledge in your mind, but also integrating it into your life so that, over time, it becomes second nature.

At first, this process will feel clunky. Just like when you first learned to drive a car, you'll be hyper-aware of everything—pausing before reacting, checking in with your emotions, and trying to remember whether to lean in or leverage. It'll take effort. But with consistent practice over time, what once felt awkward and forced will start to feel natural.

That's your goal. You're not aiming for perfection or constant self-monitoring, but slow, steady integration.

If you're anything like me when I first started this journey, you might be tempted to go all in. You might catch yourself overanalysing every feeling, dissecting every emotional cue and treating emotional intelligence like a game you need to win. I get it. When I first discovered this work, I was like a kid with a brand-new box of toys. I wanted to use every tool and every insight, all the time. I'd jump at the chance to explain emotional intelligence to my friends (whether they wanted to hear about it or not), and I'd spend way too much time analysing my own emotions, thinking that the more I examined them, the better I'd get at managing them.

Ironically, that obsession became the very thing that held me back.

Emotions aren't meant to be controlled every second of the day. They're not a puzzle to solve or a problem to fix. Sometimes, the healthiest thing you can do is just let them be. So if you ever catch yourself obsessing, pause. Breathe. Remember that progress happens over time. You don't need to be 'working on' your emotional intelligence every waking moment. In fact, trying to will only burn you out.

Think of this journey like trying to improve your fitness. If you go to the gym once, you won't suddenly be fit. But if you show up consistently, week after week, even if you don't notice it right away, change is happening.

Emotional intelligence works the same way. Every time you pause before reacting, name your emotions instead of numbing them, lean in when needed, or shift your physiological and psychological cues, you're reinforcing new neural pathways.

At first, this process will take effort. But the more you practice, the more automatic it becomes. One day, you'll realise you just handled a difficult emotion differently without even thinking about it, or you savoured an enjoyable moment or emotion. That's the moment you know it's starting to stick.

So, don't rush it. Don't force it. Just keep showing up for the practice. The more you integrate these skills into your daily life, the more naturally they'll show up when you need them most.

Chapter 3

Learning to look inwards

The second skill of happiness

If you've ever found yourself scrolling aimlessly through your phone, flicking between apps like you're searching for something without being quite sure what, you're not alone. We live in a world that demands our attention at every turn—work deadlines and family obligations vie with the endless carousel of news and social media. Even in moments of stillness, something is always ready to pull us back into the noise. We're constantly tuned in to everything except ourselves.

And yet, the research is clear: true happiness isn't found out there in the chaos. It's found in the moments we turn inward. This shift towards focusing externally in our pursuit of happiness rather than internally has not happened by accident. Your attention is an economy. Right now, some of the world's most powerful companies are locked in a battle for your focus, investing billions into ensuring you spend as much time as possible looking outward rather than inward. Social media platforms are engineered to keep you hooked. News outlets thrive on outrage and sensationalism. And advertising? Advertising is inescapable.

In 2022, a study by Raoul Bell, Laura Mieth and Axel Buchner found that New Zealand children aged between 11 and 13 years old were exposed to an average of 638 advertising messages per day—resulting in a whopping estimate of around 233 000 exposures to advertising per year. In 2024, an industry analysis by *The Ecologist* described a personal count of around 454 ads per day without spending much time using a smartphone. The same report speculated that with smartphone and social media use included, the average person could be shown thousands of ads every single day. And every one of these ads promise that happiness is just one purchase away. Perhaps a new car, a better phone, that miracle skincare routine or even a subscription service will finally make your life easier. The message is clear: if you just buy this, achieve that and upgrade here, then you'll be happy.

But here's the truth: happiness doesn't come from the next purchase, the next distraction or the next dopamine hit. It comes from something that can't be sold to you. It comes from within.

The science (and spirituality) of self-reflection and wellbeing

The field of positive psychology has been studying this for decades. Martin Seligman's PERMAH model, explored in chapter 1, suggests that introspection plays a critical role in each of the areas in the model. After all, how can you cultivate meaning, set fulfilling goals or build authentic relationships if you're not regularly checking in with yourself?

A wide range of research backs this up. Studies show that people who engage in regular self-reflection report higher levels of clarity, life satisfaction and emotional wellbeing, along with lower stress. And yet, most people don't do it—not because they don't want to, but because it's simply not a habit.

Self-reflection also isn't a modern psychological discovery. It's something philosophers and spiritual traditions have been teaching for thousands of years. Take Buddhism, for example. The practice of Vipassana meditation (which translates to 'insight' or 'special vision') is designed entirely around looking inward. It teaches that by observing our thoughts and emotions with awareness, we can gain freedom from the suffering they often bring.

The Stoics preached something similar. Marcus Aurelius, one of the greatest Stoic philosophers, journaled daily as a way to reflect on his thoughts, actions and emotions. His famous work, *Meditations,* wasn't actually written for an audience but was a private exercise in self-awareness. Even Socrates, one of history's most celebrated thinkers, declared that, 'The unexamined life is not worth living'.

In today's hyper-connected world, however, many of us have become strangers to ourselves.

If you want to build a fulfilling, contented life, you have to actually know who you are—including your values, emotions, triggers and desires. You can't just guess what makes you happy. You have to observe, explore and understand it.

This is exactly why I'm dedicating this chapter to learning the skill of looking inwards.

You've already started this journey in the previous chapter, learning to name and work with your emotions. Now, we're taking it further, using three distinct practices:

1. *Meditation and mindfulness:* To observe and understand your inner world.
2. *Journaling:* To put your thoughts into words and gain clarity.
3. *Head, heart and gut reflections:* To tap into deeper intuition and wisdom.

Note that I haven't written an exhaustive and complete account for each of these three introspection practices. I simply don't have the time or space available in the confines of one book to do so. Instead, my intention is to introduce each of these practices to you and give you the right amount of information so you can start implementing them. Of course, if you find that you end up absolutely loving some of these practices, I highly encourage you to continue learning about them via other books and resources. But for now, the most important thing is to get curious about how you can utilise each of these practices as a tool to help you tune out the noise of the world and tune into yourself.

Because happiness isn't found in the next scroll, the next distraction or the next external achievement. It's found in the moments you pause, look inward and truly see yourself.

Meditation and mindfulness

Picture this: you finally carve out a few minutes to try meditation. You sit down, cross your legs, close your eyes and take a deep breath. And, immediately, your brain goes into overdrive. *Did I send that email? What's for dinner? My back hurts. Wait, am I doing this right?* You suddenly become acutely aware of how loud your mind is. It's like a toddler on a sugar high. It feels anything but calming. And, like so many people, you decide that meditation 'just isn't for you'.

I get it. We're wired for constant stimulation. We fill every quiet moment with background noise—scrolling, streaming, texting and talking. So much so that when we finally do stop and sit with ourselves, it can feel uncomfortable and even confronting.

But here's the thing: that discomfort is the reason meditation and mindfulness are so powerful. They teach us to get comfortable with ourselves, and to sit with our thoughts without trying to fight them, drown them out or run away from them.

And if you stick with it, even just for a few minutes a day, meditation can change your life in ways you never expected.

A practice older than time (almost)

Meditation isn't some trendy wellness hack. It's been around for thousands of years. Ancient Hindu texts describe meditation as a path to higher consciousness. Buddhist traditions centre on mindfulness (sati), which teaches awareness of thoughts, feelings and sensations without attachment. Taoist practices in China, as well as Christian and Islamic contemplative traditions, all share similar themes: turning inward, observing the mind, and cultivating a sense of peace and clarity.

Fast-forward to today, and science is finally catching up with what ancient wisdom has long known. Research has proven that learning to sit with your mind is one of the best things you can do for your happiness.

If meditation came in pill form, it would probably be the most prescribed medication in history. The benefits are that compelling. And yet, instead of swallowing a tablet, all you need to do is sit, breathe and pay attention. Simple, right? Well, yes and no. But before I get into why meditation can feel like an uphill battle at first, let's talk about why it's worth pushing through the initial resistance.

For decades, researchers have been fascinated by what happens to the brain and body when we meditate, and the results are staggering.

Meditation has been shown to lower cortisol levels (that lovely stress hormone responsible for making you feel on edge and snappy). It activates the parasympathetic nervous system—your body's built-in relaxation switch—helping you move out of fight-or-flight mode and into a calmer state. Studies on mindfulness-based stress reduction (MBSR), a program developed by Dr Jon Kabat-Zinn, have found that just eight weeks of mindfulness practice can significantly reduce stress and anxiety levels. Eight weeks. After two months of consistently showing up and sitting with yourself, your brain literally rewires itself to handle stress better.

And speaking of rewiring, meditation is like strength training for your brain. Regular practice actually increases the size of the prefrontal cortex, the area responsible for decision-making, focus and impulse control. At the same time, it reduces activity in the amygdala, the fear centre of your brain. What does that mean in everyday life? It means you're less reactive, less likely to spiral into overthinking and more in control of your emotions. In short, you don't sweat the small stuff as much.

Then there's the happiness factor. Studies have found that mindfulness increases dopamine and serotonin—those feel-good brain chemicals linked to contentment and overall wellbeing. MRI scans have even shown that long-term meditators have more grey matter in the areas of the brain associated with emotional regulation and self-awareness. And the more grey matter, the stronger and more developed that part of the brain becomes.

But it's not just your mind that benefits. Meditation has been linked to better sleep, increased creativity, a stronger immune system and even reduced inflammation in the body. Some studies suggest it can even help with pain management, making it a natural alternative for those looking to reduce reliance on medication.

No wonder some of the most successful and high-performing people in the world swear by it.

Getting 'good' at meditation

So if meditation is so life-changing, why isn't everyone doing it? Because, let's be honest, it's not easy. The idea of sitting still and doing 'nothing' sounds blissful in theory. In practice, it's like trying to tame a wild monkey with a megaphone. The moment you sit down, your mind will likely start listing all the things you should be doing instead. You'll suddenly remember emails you forgot to reply to, meals you want to cook and embarrassing things you said in high school. You might even feel restless or frustrated, convinced you're 'doing it wrong'.

The truth is no-one is naturally 'good' at meditation. As with any skill, it takes practice. And that's where a lot of people get stuck.

For starters, meditation is new to most of us. Remember the four stages of skill development I covered in chapter 1? When you first start meditating, you're firmly in stage one—unconscious incompetence. You don't even realise how much your mind controls you until you sit down and try to observe it. Then, as you move into conscious incompetence, it becomes glaringly obvious that your mind is a hyperactive toddler on a sugar high. This stage can be uncomfortable, but it's a necessary part of the process.

Then there's the fact that sitting with your thoughts, without distraction, is confronting. We live in a world that encourages constant stimulation through scrolling, binge-watching and other background noise. The moment you strip all that away, you come face to face with what's actually going on inside your head. That can feel overwhelming at first, but here's the thing: leaning into discomfort is how you grow.

And let's not forget the perfection trap. Too many people think they have to meditate for an hour a day, sitting cross-legged in complete silence, with their mind completely empty. That's like saying you have to run a marathon to be a runner. In reality, a few minutes a day is enough to start reaping the benefits. The key is consistency, not intensity.

Bringing meditation and mindfulness into everyday life

If the idea of sitting in stillness for 20 minutes makes you want to crawl out of your own skin, here's some good news: you don't have to.

Meditation isn't just something you do in a quiet room with incense burning and Tibetan bells chiming in the background. Mindfulness can be woven into your daily life, no matter how busy you are. Try the following:

- *Mindful eating:* Instead of mindlessly scrolling on your phone while eating, take time to actually taste your food. Notice the textures, the flavours and the act of chewing.
- *Walking meditation:* Next time you go for a walk, leave your phone in your pocket and actually notice your surroundings. Feel your feet on the ground and listen to the sounds around you.
- *Breath awareness:* At any point in the day, take ten seconds to check in with your breath. Is it shallow? Deep? Slow?

Fast? A few intentional deep breaths can instantly shift your nervous system.

- *Shinrin-yoku (forest bathing):* This is a Japanese practice that involves immersing yourself in nature and engaging your senses fully. Without an agenda or your phone, just be present in the environment.
- *Guided meditation:* If sitting in silence feels overwhelming, apps such as Headspace, Calm and Insight Timer provide guided meditations that walk you through the process.

You don't need to dedicate hours to meditation to feel its effects. Even a few moments of mindfulness throughout your day can rewire your brain, lower stress and increase happiness.

Reflection and application

Meditation is a lot like exercise. You don't have to be good at it to benefit from it. You just have to do it.

So, here's your challenge for the next week:

1. *Pick a practice:* Choose one mindfulness technique that feels doable. It could be two minutes of deep breathing before bed or a short, guided meditation in the morning.
2. *Make it easy:* Don't overcomplicate it. Attach meditation to something you already do, like making your morning coffee or brushing your teeth.
3. *Drop the perfectionism:* 'Failing' at meditation isn't possible. Some days your mind will be restless, and that's okay. What matters is that you show up.

That's it. You've meditated.

(continued)

Do this once a day for a week. If two minutes feels good, try five. If five feels good, try ten. But don't overthink it and don't make it a chore. Just show up, breathe and notice. You might be surprised by what happens next.

Remember — the real benefits of meditation aren't in the minutes you spend sitting in stillness. They come in how you show up for yourself, your loved ones and the world once you open your eyes.

Journaling

Have you ever had a thought looping in your mind like a song you can't turn off? Maybe it's an idea you can't quite figure out, an emotion you don't fully understand or a frustration that keeps bubbling to the surface.

Now, imagine if you could pull that thought out of your head, lay it down in front of you and see it for what it really is. You could transform it from something chaotic and overwhelming into something you can make sense of and work with; something that, just maybe, has been trying to tell you something all along.

For centuries, humans have turned to the blank page to process their inner worlds. Marcus Aurelius scribbled down his reflections on wisdom and virtue in what would later be known as *Meditations*. Anne Frank found solace in her diary, confiding in it as if it were a trusted friend. Leonardo da Vinci's notebooks were an explosion of ideas, blending art, science and philosophy in a way that only his mind could.

Journaling isn't just for philosophers, writers or those living through history's most challenging moments. It's for anyone who wants to untangle their thoughts, gain clarity and get to know themselves a little better.

If meditation is about sitting with yourself, journaling is about talking to yourself—and learning to listen.

As already acknowledged, our minds are noisy places. On any given day, we cycle through tens of thousands of thoughts. Many of these thoughts are repetitive or unhelpful, and almost all of them are competing for attention.

Left unchecked, those thoughts pile up, creating mental clutter. But when you write them down, something powerful happens. Journaling is like emptying a messy drawer. At first, everything spills out and it looks even worse than before. But then, as you sift through, you start sorting things out, throwing away what doesn't serve you and making sense of the things that do.

Writing externalises your thoughts, taking them out of the swirling mess in your head and making them tangible. You can examine them, challenge them, or simply put them down so they're no longer bouncing around and demanding your attention.

Journaling is a tool for emotional processing, a way of decluttering the mind and, perhaps most importantly, a chance to see patterns you might not have noticed before. Maybe you always feel irritable on Sunday nights. Maybe certain worries keep showing up in different disguises. Maybe the things that stress you out the most aren't the things you thought they were.

Journaling helps you connect the dots between your thoughts, emotions and behaviours. And once you see the patterns, you can start shifting them.

The science of why journaling makes you happier

Beyond the anecdotal benefits, science backs up the power of journaling. Studies have found that expressive writing—particularly about emotions—reduces activity in the amygdala (the brain's fear centre), making us less reactive to stress. Like meditation, it's also been shown to lower cortisol (the stress hormone) and improve immune function.

Journaling is linked to greater emotional intelligence, helping people regulate their emotions more effectively and reduce rumination (that exhausting cycle of overthinking). Research from the University of Rochester highlights that journaling helps individuals process complex feelings, leading to reduced anxiety and depression.

And it doesn't just help with the heavy stuff. Gratitude journaling, for instance, has been found to significantly boost happiness levels, rewiring the brain to focus on what's good, rather than what's missing. People who journal regularly about what they're grateful for report feeling more optimistic and satisfied with life—even months later. Hold that thought for now—because I explore gratitude much more deeply in the next chapter.

Breaking through resistance to journaling

Now, I can already hear some of your reasons for not journaling:

- 'I wouldn't know what to write.'
- 'I don't have time.'
- 'I tried it once, and it didn't work.'

I get it. The idea of writing down your thoughts can feel awkward, unnecessary or even uncomfortable at first. But let's be real: how often do you actually sit down and check in with yourself? It's easy to keep moving through life, reacting to whatever comes your way, without ever stopping to ask, 'How do I actually feel about this? What do I really want?'

Journaling isn't about being a good writer. It's about giving yourself space to think, feel and process.

If you don't know what to write, start by writing exactly that. 'I don't know what to write' is, ironically, a great way to get started. Because somewhere after that sentence, your real thoughts will start trickling through.

If you don't think you have time, try it for five minutes. Nobody I've coached has ever sat down for five minutes of journaling and regretted it.

If you've tried before and it didn't work, consider that maybe you just hadn't found your way of journaling yet. More than one way to do this is possible.

Few people enjoy staring at a blank page. The key is finding a style that works for you. Here are a few approaches to try:

- *Stream-of-consciousness journaling:* Write whatever comes to mind—no filter and no overthinking. This can be a great way to declutter your brain.
- *Gratitude journaling:* Reflect on what you're grateful for. This helps shift your focus to the positive and trains your brain to notice joy.
- *Reflective journaling:* Look back on your day and explore what went well, what didn't and what you learned.
- *Prompted journaling:* Use specific questions to guide your reflections. (See the 'Reflection and application' box towards the end of this section for some great prompts to get started.)

- *Bullet journaling:* Use a mix of lists, reflections and goal-setting, all in a structured format. This can be great for those who love organisation.
- *Audio journaling:* Prefer talking over writing? Record voice notes instead.

If you're going to do this, make it easy for yourself:

- Keep a notebook by your bed or simply open a Google Doc.
- Set a reminder.
- Remember that you don't have to write every day, but the more often you do it, the more you'll notice the benefits.
- Forget perfection. No-one is grading this. Some days, you'll write one sentence. Other days, you'll go on a rant that fills three pages. Both are completely fine.

The goal isn't to write something profound. The goal is to give your thoughts and feelings somewhere to go.

Reflection and application

To help you get started with journaling, here are a few prompts to try:

- 'What's been on my mind a lot lately?'
- 'If my emotions could talk right now, what would they say?'
- 'What's one thing I've learned about myself in the last month?'
- 'What's something small I can appreciate about today?'
- 'What do I need to let go of right now?'

Your thoughts deserve space. Your emotions deserve to be acknowledged. Your story deserves to be written—if only for you. So, grab a notebook, open a blank document or hit record on a voice note. And just start.

Head, heart and gut reflections

Have you ever felt completely torn over a decision? Like different parts of you were waging war inside your head, each convinced they were right? Maybe you had been offered an exciting new job, but while part of you was saying, 'This is an incredible opportunity!', another part was whispering, 'But what if you fail?', and a third, quieter part was murmuring something you couldn't quite make out.

This internal conflict isn't just frustrating but also exhausting. It can leave you stuck in a loop of overthinking, second-guessing and, ultimately, procrastinating. Perhaps you've pushed through in the past and made a decision, only to later wonder if you should have gone the other way. Or perhaps you avoided making a choice altogether, hoping clarity would magically appear. *Spoiler alert:* It usually doesn't.

What if, instead of trying to force clarity, you could simply listen more intentionally? That's where head, heart and gut journaling comes in. This practice isn't about forcing yourself to pick a side or silencing your doubts. It's about checking in with the different parts of yourself, understanding their concerns, and making decisions that are aligned, informed and deeply authentic.

Your inner decision-making panel: The head, the heart and the gut

Three core internal voices shape your decisions. These come from:

- *The head:* The logical, analytical thinker that prioritises safety, planning and rationality.
- *The heart:* The emotional, passionate dreamer that prioritises happiness, connection and what feels good.
- *The gut:* The deep, intuitive knowing that prioritises authenticity, alignment and truth.

The way these three voices come together to form your internal decision-making panel is shown in the following figure.

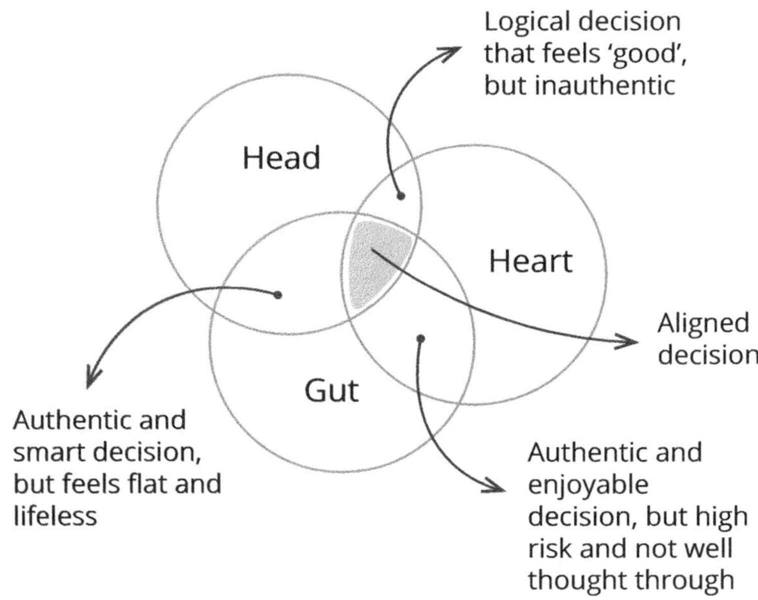

Your inner decision-making panel

Most of us live almost exclusively in our heads, occasionally consulting our hearts, but rarely tuning into our gut. This is because the head is loud and relentless, the heart is often impulsive, and the gut—our most reliable internal compass—is quiet and easy to ignore.

Think of these voices as being like different members of a meeting. Your head bursts into the room, waving spreadsheets and rattling off statistics about why this decision is too risky. Your heart swoops in dramatically, talking about how this feels like the right choice. And your gut? Your gut is sitting at the back of the room, arms crossed, waiting for someone to ask it what it thinks.

The goal is to learn to live from the gut up, rather than the head down.

Understanding the role of each voice

Before I dive into each of the three voices, it's worth noting that they all serve distinct but interconnected roles. While they can sometimes feel like they're in conflict, each voice is trying to guide you toward safety, authenticity or fulfilment. They just try to get there in different ways. By getting to know the role and rhythm of each one, you can better understand how to navigate decisions, challenges and everyday life with greater self-awareness and alignment.

The head: The survival strategist

Your head's primary job is keeping you alive. It's why you look both ways before crossing the street, why you hesitate before making big changes, and why you weigh pros and cons before taking a leap.

The head values certainty. It resists risk, thrives on logic and prefers the comfort of the familiar. This tendency is useful in many ways. It helps us plan, problem-solve and avoid genuinely bad decisions. But if left unchecked, it can also keep us trapped in our comfort zones.

Ever had an exciting idea, only to talk yourself out of it with 'rational' concerns? That's your head at work, trying to maintain the status quo.

The heart: The passionate dreamer

If your head is the strategist, your heart is the adventurer. It's driven by joy, excitement and the pursuit of happiness. It's the part of you that falls in love with new ideas, takes spontaneous trips and follows what feels right.

But while the heart is essential for passion and connection, it can also be impulsive and short-sighted. It's the part of you that says, 'Quit your job! Move to Bali! Start a business!', without necessarily considering the long-term consequences.

Without guidance from the head and gut, the heart can lead you to chase fleeting desires rather than deep fulfilment.

The gut: The quiet compass

If the head is a loud debater and the heart is an enthusiastic storyteller, the gut is the wise elder who doesn't waste words. It doesn't yell. It doesn't argue. It just knows.

Unlike the head (which fears change) and the heart (which craves excitement), the gut is concerned with authenticity. It whispers when something is out of alignment. It nudges you toward decisions that reflect your true self.

But here's the catch: you have to be quiet enough to hear it.

Most people ignore their gut because it doesn't provide spreadsheets or emotional fireworks. Instead, it just offers a deep, steady knowing.

If you've ever had a moment where something 'just didn't feel right' but you couldn't explain why, that was your gut.

The battle for control

Each of these voices wants to be in charge, even if in sometimes subtle ways:

- The head wants to call the shots because it's 'logical'.
- The heart wants to lead because it's 'passionate'.
- The gut doesn't fight for control, but when ignored, you feel lost, misaligned and disconnected from yourself.

The goal of this practice is to rebalance the dynamic between your head, heart and gut, making space for all of your inner voices so they work together, rather than against each other.

Head, heart and gut journaling is a simple way to turn inner conflict into inner collaboration. Here's how it works:

1. Choose a decision or challenge you're currently facing.
2. Write separate responses from each of your inner voices:
   - *Head:* What is my logical mind saying about this? What are the risks, pros and cons?
   - *Heart:* What excites me? What scares me? What do I feel pulled towards?
   - *Gut:* What does my deep instinct say? If I sit in stillness, what knowing arises?

Once you've written everything out—including perspectives from your head, heart and gut—take a moment to step back and read through what you've captured. As you do, you might start to notice a few patterns.

Your head may be filled with fear-based reasoning, offering logical arguments that are focused on safety and caution. Your heart might be leading with excitement and possibility, but without much of a practical plan to follow through. Then there's your gut, often the quietest voice in the room, quietly offering something simple and powerful that you may have overlooked.

When you give each part of yourself a voice, you can begin to see the full picture of what's happening inside. Rather than feeling like you're being pulled in different directions, you now have a clearer understanding of your internal dialogue and how each part of you is trying to help in its own way.

The goal isn't to blindly follow one voice. The goal is to integrate them. Maybe your gut says yes, but your head needs a better plan. Great! Now you can take inspired action without feeling reckless.

Reflection and application

Think about your past decisions. What percentage of your life have you spent letting your head take the lead? What about your heart or your gut?

If your head has dominated, you might have played it safe, hesitated on risks or struggled with overthinking.

If your heart has led the way, you might have followed excitement but lacked direction.

If your gut has been ignored, you might feel like you've been living someone else's life rather than your own.

Write about it. Get curious. See what patterns emerge.

Living from the gut up

As I've mentioned, most people let their head make all their decisions, check in with their heart occasionally, and completely ignore their gut. But true clarity comes when you listen to all parts of yourself. Your head is smart. Your heart is passionate. Your gut is wise.

When you integrate your three inner voices, you stop feeling torn. You stop second-guessing. You start making decisions that feel aligned—not just smart or exciting, but right. The answers are already inside you. You just need to start listening.

If you take one thing from this chapter, I hope it's this: happiness isn't something you trip over while going about your life. You don't just wake up one day and think, *Ah, there it is. Found it!* Happiness is something you cultivate, like a garden. And introspection is the sunlight, the water and the soil. It's what allows you to grow something real, something lasting and something that feels deeply aligned to you as an individual.

In this chapter, I've outlined some of the most powerful tools for looking inward. Meditation and mindfulness teach you how to get out of your own head (ironically, by diving straight into it). Journaling shows you how to get your tangled thoughts onto paper, where you can actually make sense of them. And head, heart and gut check-ins help you listen to the three main voices competing for control of your life—and get them working together instead of arguing like siblings on a long road trip.

But here's the thing: introspection isn't just a nice skill to have. It's essential. Because if you don't take the time to understand yourself—including your emotions, your thoughts and your inner compass—you'll spend your whole life reacting to the world instead of actually choosing how you want to live in it. And when it comes to happiness, the difference between reacting and choosing is the difference between feeling like life is something that just happens to you and feeling like it's something you're actively shaping.

Now, don't get me wrong. This doesn't mean you need to become some enlightened monk, spending hours a day in meditation, writing 20-page journal entries about your childhood, or checking in with your head, heart and gut before deciding what sandwich to order. (Although, let's be honest, some lunch choices do feel existential.)

It simply means making space—a few minutes here, a quiet reflection there—to pause, check in and reconnect with yourself. It means choosing to look inward, even when the world is shouting at you to keep scrolling, keep consuming and keep running. It means trusting that your happiness isn't something to be found 'out there' in the next big achievement, purchase or distraction, but something that's already within you, waiting to be nurtured.

Carl Jung once said, 'Who looks outside dreams; who looks inside awakens'. So, as I close this chapter, I want to leave you with one question: are you ready to wake up?

Chapter 4

Retraining your brain

The third skill of happiness

Have you ever noticed how your brain is an expert at pointing out everything that's going wrong? You could have a hundred things going well—your morning coffee was just the right temperature, your boss gave you positive feedback, the sun is shining—and, yet, if one thing goes wrong, that's what your brain latches onto. Your barista gets your order wrong? Ruins the whole morning. Someone cuts you off in traffic? Suddenly, humanity is doomed. You send a text and don't get a reply for a few hours? Clearly, you've been abandoned forever, and no-one loves you anymore.

This isn't you being a pessimist. It's not even necessarily you being dramatic (though, let's be honest, we all have our moments). This is your brain doing exactly what it has evolved to do. It's called the 'negative cognitive bias', and it's one of the brain's oldest and most deeply ingrained survival mechanisms.

Our ancestors, those scrappy, survival-focused early humans, weren't too concerned about enjoying life. They weren't waking up thinking, *I should really take some time to practice gratitude for this beautiful sunrise.* No, they were waking up thinking, *What could kill me today?* And that hyper-focus on danger kept them alive. The ones who were constantly scanning for threats, the ones who noticed the rustling in the bushes before anyone else did, were the ones who survived long enough to pass on their genes.

The problem is that same survival system is still running in your brain today, even though your daily threats are more about overdue bills and workplace deadlines than lurking predators. Your mind is still wired to focus on problems, scan for danger and react more strongly to what's wrong than what's right.

And here's where things get tricky. Not only does your brain naturally lean towards the negative, but the world around you feeds that tendency. A key approach from traditional media has always been, 'If it bleeds, it leads'. Social media is now full of highlight reels that make you feel like your life isn't good enough compared to everyone else's. And your own thoughts are often a greatest-hits album of every mistake, awkward moment and failure you've ever had.

You've probably been experiencing some of this negative cognitive bias throughout the earlier chapters of this book, even if you haven't realised it. When you tried meditating, for example, you likely noticed that your mind wandered toward worries and problems faster than it drifted toward gratitude. When you started journaling, you may have found it easier to vent frustrations than to reflect on moments of joy. And when you explored your head, heart and gut, chances are you realised that your head—the part of you wired for survival—had a much louder voice than the other two.

But, despite how I may have started the chapter, this isn't all doom and gloom. I do have good news: while your brain may have evolved for survival, it's also able to change.

Neuroplasticity: Your brain is more changeable than you think

For most of human history, scientists believed that (at least after childhood) the brain was like a fully developed machine. It was static, unchangeable and set in stone by the time you reached adulthood. It was this kind of thinking that promoted IQ as the greatest pursuit of humanity, and that gave us such historical flops as phrenology—the idea that personality, intelligence and someone's character could be determined by their head shape and size. (Because, obviously, that correlates to the shape and size of their brain. In case you didn't catch it, that 'obviously' was dripping in sarcasm—I literally rolled my own eyes when writing the definition of phrenology. Anyway, back to our story.)

Thankfully, science didn't stay stuck on the idea that our brain is a 'set and forget' kind of asset. Along came the discovery of neuroplasticity, which showed that the brain isn't actually a fixed structure at all. It's more like a muscle. And, importantly, it can rewire, adapt and grow based on what you practise.

Think of your neural pathways as being like hiking trails. The more you think a certain way, the stronger and deeper that trail becomes. If you're constantly dwelling on the negative, for example, you're reinforcing that path, making it easier for your brain to go there automatically. But, like many a bold and intrepid hiker in history has shown us, you don't have to stick to the well-worn paths. You can intentionally build new paths in your brain—ones that lead to more balanced and more optimistic thinking, for example.

Does this mean you ignore problems? No. This isn't about slapping on a fake smile and pretending everything is fine. This is about expanding your perspective so that you see the whole picture—the good and the bad. It's about balancing out that ancient survival mechanism with a more accurate view of reality.

And this brings me to the goal of this chapter. I'm going to help you train your brain to be better at noticing the good. I don't mean this in a toxic positivity, 'good vibes only' kind of way, but in a way that helps you feel more balanced, more in control and more deeply connected to the genuinely nice moments in your life.

In this chapter, I explore three key practices that will help you retrain your brain for happiness:

1. *Gratitude training:* This is actively practising gratitude to rewire your brain's natural tendency to fixate on problems. (No, this doesn't mean keeping a Pinterest-perfect gratitude journal that you feel guilty for never writing in. This means real, practical strategies that actually work.)
2. *Rethinking expectations:* Once you understand how rigid expectations lead to disappointment, frustration and stress, you can start looking at the antidote: appreciation.
3. *Perspective shifting:* This is learning how to challenge and reshape negative thought patterns with simple but powerful mental exercises.

These aren't just fluffy self-help concepts. They're backed by decades of research in psychology and neuroscience. Similar to other tools already discussed (such as self-reflection, labelling emotions and meditation), studies have shown that gratitude literally rewires the brain, increasing activity in the prefrontal cortex (the area responsible for decision-making and perspective-taking) while decreasing activity in the amygdala (the fear centre). Practising gratitude regularly can reduce cortisol (the stress hormone), increase dopamine and serotonin (the 'feel-good' chemicals), and even improve sleep and immune function. One study from researchers Robert Emmons and Michael McCullough found that people who kept a gratitude journal for just three weeks reported significantly higher wellbeing and lower levels of depression compared to those who didn't. Other research has found that people who regularly practice gratitude experience higher levels of life satisfaction.

And when it comes to happiness, expectations can be both a gift and a trap. Psychologists have long studied what's called the 'expectation gap'—the emotional space between what we expect to happen and what actually unfolds. The wider the gap when reality falls below expectations, the greater our feelings of disappointment, frustration and dissatisfaction. So it's not just reality that impacts our happiness, but also how reality compares to the version we had imagined in our minds.

Interestingly, research shows that those who practice appreciation over expectation report higher levels of resilience, joy and overall wellbeing. By shifting focus from what 'should' happen to what is happening, you can experience greater contentment, even when life doesn't go exactly to plan. This isn't about giving up hope or ambition. It's about learning to find value and meaning in what's real, rather than chasing an ever-moving target of perfection.

A similar perspective shift can occur in the way we categorise events. We tend to label events as 'good' or 'bad' based on our immediate emotional response. However, we can shift this to a more balanced perspective using what I call 'worst-case, best-case and most likely case thinking'. In doing so, we can reduce the catastrophising and increase clarity.

Here's the bottom line of what the science about neuroplasticity tells us: your brain is not your enemy, but it does often need a little retraining if you want to become the happiest version of yourself.

Sure, your brain will always be wired to notice the problems first, to cling to the negative and to react more strongly to pain than to pleasure. That's just how the human mind works. But with the right tools, you can shift those patterns. You can train your brain to also notice what's good, to savour joy and to widen your perspective beyond just survival-mode thinking.

So let's get started. Because once you learn to rewire your brain for happiness, the world doesn't change, but how you see it does. And that changes everything.

Gratitude: The art of noticing the good

For years, I wanted to be the kind of person who had a rock-solid gratitude practice. You know the type. The ones who wake up at 5 am, sip their green tea and effortlessly jot down profound reflections on all the beauty in their life. That was not me.

I tried. Oh, I tried. I bought fancy journals with gold-embossed covers that promised to change my life in five minutes a day. I committed to writing three things I was grateful for every night. And, for about a week, I felt like I was on the fast track to enlightenment.

I wanted to be one of those people who effortlessly exuded gratitude. I wanted to radiate warmth, notice the tiny joys in life and somehow find a way to be grateful for traffic because it gave me a chance to listen to an audiobook. Basically, I wanted to be a living, breathing, Disney character that sung to birds in the morning. (Because does that person actually exist?)

But every time I sat down to 'practise gratitude', I hit a wall. After a few days of dedication, it would just kind of stop feeling good. So I'd stop doing it. Eventually, after years of learning more about gratitude and its role in supporting happiness, I realised that I'd been making two critical errors with my gratitude practice.

To start with, I was always starting from scratch. I'd open my journal, pen poised, ready to pour out my heart, only to be met with absolute silence. My brain, so full of thoughts every other minute of the day, suddenly had nothing to say. It was like trying to think of a clever joke on the spot or a 'fun fact' about yourself during those hell-forsaken icebreaker activities. I had nothing but static running through my brain. The blank page stared at me, waiting. I tried the obvious ones. 'I'm grateful for my family.' 'I'm grateful for food.' 'I'm grateful for a roof over my head.' They were all true. But they were also painfully generic. And none of them really sparked anything in me that felt genuine.

And this dovetails nicely into my second problem. I was only scratching the surface with my gratitude practice. I just wasn't going deep enough. I'd heard all about the benefits of gratitude, and read the studies that showed it could rewire the brain, improve mental health and even boost physical wellbeing. But my attempts felt robotic. I felt like I was merely checking off a box on my ever-growing personal development to-do list: write three things, nod in vague satisfaction and move on with my day.

There was no depth or real feeling to it. I felt like I was going through the motions at the gym but never breaking a sweat. Technically, I was doing the thing. 'I'm grateful for ... breakfast, I guess?' But was it actually making a difference? Not really.

Then, after months of abandoning and revisiting the practice, I stumbled onto something that changed everything. Admittedly, that sounds pretty dramatic but I honestly do credit this simple change as being the thing that finally got me into practising gratitude.

Instead of staring at a blank page and hoping inspiration would strike, I started using a simple template with three prompt questions that guided me to a more meaningful, emotionally connected sense of gratitude.

Using a gratitude template

Here's a run through of my personal gratitude practice template (and, yes, I encourage you to steal it and use it).

Gratitude for the little moments

First, I started asking myself, 'What's something small that I'd usually overlook and take for granted, but today I'm going to appreciate?' This one was important because it forced me to zoom in and notice the tiny moments that might otherwise go unnoticed.

Maybe it was the way the morning sun hit my face through the kitchen window or an expected smile from a passing stranger. These were small things, but that was the point. Gratitude isn't just for the big, obvious moments. It doesn't have to be some big song and dance. You can find plenty to be grateful for in the 'day in and day out'. We just need to give those moments a little more attention.

Gratitude for others

Then I would answer the second prompt: 'Who is someone I feel grateful for today?' Word of warning: if you do this one right, it is a real heartwarmer. For me, it made gratitude feel relational and connected. It made it about someone else other than just me.

Sometimes, I was grateful for someone close to me like my wife or a close friend. Other times, I was grateful for someone I barely knew but who had made a small difference in my day—perhaps a staff member at a local restaurant who remembered my favourite order, or the person who slowed down to let me merge in traffic when they absolutely didn't have to.

Over time, I found that when gratitude is directed towards other people, it has a beautiful way of making us all feel a little less alone and little more connected—and a lot more happy.

Gratitude for self

And then came the toughest one. To this day, whenever I teach people these three gratitude prompts I give them the heads-up that this prompt is the most challenging, but in many ways also the most beneficial. I think that's why I would always leave it to last. I needed to warm up my gratitude muscles before attempting the big gratitude question: 'What is something about me that I'm grateful for?'

This was the hardest prompt for me because, like most people, I had spent years perfecting the art of being my own worst critic. It felt unnatural to look inwards with appreciation rather than judgement. But the more I practised it, the more I realised how much I had been overlooking. As it turned out, I actually have plenty of qualities I like about myself.

Some days, I was grateful for my perseverance. Every so often, I'd be grateful for my knowledge and insight. Other days, I kept it light. I once wrote that I was grateful my beard wasn't patchy. It didn't really matter what I wrote, the only thing that mattered was that I was training my brain to acknowledge and appreciate myself, rather than criticise myself. At the time, this was something I had never really done before.

The bonus step: Marinating in gratitude

Once I had my three answers for the day, I started experimenting with adding in one extra step. I'd ask myself, 'Why?'

Why, out of all the small things in my day, was that the one little moment that stood out enough to write down? Why, out of all the people I encountered, was that the person I felt grateful for? Why, out of all the traits I could have focused on in myself, did I choose that one?

This extra step of revisiting my answers and asking 'why' turned gratitude from a mental exercise into an actual feeling. It forced me to sit with this feeling, to let it sink in and actually experience the sensation of being grateful. I often call this part of the practice 'marinating in gratitude'. And that's where the real benefits started showing up.

Over time, something interesting began to happen. I found myself noticing things I might have ignored before. My brain, once so good at scanning for problems, started scanning for moments of appreciation. Life didn't suddenly become perfect. In fact, at that time in my life, not much had changed externally at all. My brain was just getting better at actually noticing all the good things that had been there all along.

The shift wasn't dramatic. I didn't wake up one day to a big beam of light shining down from the heavens and blessing me with the almighty power of being grateful. The shift was much more subtle, like adjusting the brightness on a screen. But that subtle shift made one hell of a difference.

Like anybody else, I still experience hard days. But even on those days, I'm now much better at finding one small thing. And once I find one, I can usually find another. Over time, these grateful little moments stack up and, slowly but surely, the hard days don't seem as all-consumingly shit as they once did. Even on the hard days, I'm able to experience a bit of happiness.

Gratitude is contagious

In his 2013 TED Talk (appropriately titled, 'Want to be happy? Be grateful'), David Steindl-Rast shares the following: 'It is not happiness that makes us grateful, but gratefulness that makes us happy'.

Now, I've just spent a few pages telling you all about how much gratitude improved my personal sense of happiness. This should come as no surprise, but I did so with the explicit intent that you would feel encouraged to practise gratitude for your own personal happiness.

But the good news just keeps coming—because it turns out that gratitude is about much more than our happiness as individuals. Gratitude is contagious.

Think about the last time someone genuinely thanked you—not in a passing 'Thanks for that', but in a way that made you feel seen and appreciated. How'd you feel afterwards? Dare I say you likely felt pretty chuffed—perhaps, even, a bit happier.

What about when you noticed someone being genuinely grateful for a meal they were having, or someone deeply enjoying music at a live concert? I'm willing to bet that when you've seen someone exercising the practice of gratitude, or experiencing the feeling of gratitude, it's sparked a little something in you. And that something has made you feel a little more grateful too.

It's a pretty powerful thing, isn't it?

This brings me to one of the best things you can possibly do if you want to solidify your gratitude practice: share it. If you're grateful for someone, tell them. Send the text. Make the call. Walk up to them and say it. If you enjoyed a meal or some live music, let people know. We all need to be way more active about celebrating good things in life.

Yes, it might feel a little awkward at first. We're not used to expressing appreciation so openly. But I promise you, no-one has ever been upset about being genuinely thanked.

And here's the kicker: expressing gratitude won't just make the other person feel good. It'll make you feel good, too. It deepens your relationships, strengthens connections and reinforces the habit of noticing what's good. And this is why I regularly emphasise the following whenever I speak about gratitude: 'Gratitude shared is gratitude doubled'.

As we reach the end of this section on gratitude, I hope you take away the lesson that gratitude is not a fluffy, roll your eyes, hashtag kind of thing that influencers use on social media. It's a deeply impactful commitment to help your brain see the good that's already right there in front of you.

Start small. Don't try to do it perfectly. Some days, you'll forget. Some days, it will feel forced. That's okay. The goal isn't perfection. The goal is simply to start.

And if you ever find yourself staring at a blank page, unsure of what to write, just ask yourself:

- 'What's something small I appreciate today?'
- 'Who am I grateful for?'
- 'What's something about myself I can appreciate?'

Most importantly, ask yourself why?

Reflection and application

Here's how to get started with gratitude journaling:

1. Get yourself a gratitude journal. It can be a physical journal or a gratitude app.
2. Decide on three prompts to use when you're not sure what to be grateful for. You are more than welcome to steal my three, or come up with your own. If they eventually feel stale, change them up.
3. Every day for at least the next month, spend ten to 15 minutes writing down what you're grateful for and *why*. (And, let's be real — what I mean when I say 'every day' is aim for a 75 per cent success rate.)
4. Go out of your way to share gratitude with others. Thank someone, write someone a nice message, or call an old friend and tell them what you appreciate about them.

Expectation: The thief of joy

It starts innocently enough. You plan a holiday, imagining yourself lying on a pristine beach, cocktail in hand, the sun setting in an explosion of warm oranges and pinks. It's going to be perfect. You can already feel the relaxation seeping into your bones. Then, reality hits. And it hits you hard.

Your flight gets delayed. The resort isn't as dreamy as it looked online. Your partner wants to go hiking instead of lounging by the pool and—just to really top things off—it starts raining. Of course it does. Before you've even ordered a cocktail, let alone had a sip of one, the relaxation you expected turns into frustration.

This is the power of expectations. When reality falls short of the grand mental picture we've painted, disappointment swoops in like an uninvited guest, eating all the snacks and refusing to leave.

Perhaps you've heard the proverb (often misattributed to Shakespeare), 'Expectation is the root of all heartache'. If you look around, you'll notice it rings true in almost every area of life.

We expect our careers to progress in a neat upward trajectory. We expect our relationships to be full of romance and free from conflict. We expect our coffee order to be made exactly the way we like it. And when life inevitably refuses to comply with our meticulously crafted mental script, we feel cheated, let down and sometimes even downright angry.

This is not at all to say that having hopes, goals or standards is a bad thing. But a fine line exists between aspiration and expectation. Aspiration says, 'This would be amazing and I'll work toward it'. Expectation says, 'This is how it should be, and if it's not, I'm upset'. One is motivating. The other is a complete gamble between happiness and disappointment.

The psychology of expectations

From an evolutionary standpoint, expectations make a lot of sense—they're not just your brain setting you up for a bad time. They once served us well. Predictability meant survival. If our ancestors expected the seasons to change, they could prepare and plant the right crops. If they expected a rustling in the bushes to be a predator, they lived to see another day. But in the modern world, our expectations often work against us.

We don't just predict outcomes; we preload them with emotional weight. Studies show that when people expect something to make them happy, such as a promotion, a holiday or even a new phone, they experience a temporary spike in excitement. But once they get the thing? The emotional high fades faster than you can say 'new iPhone release'. This is called the 'impact bias', and it tricks us into believing that future events or achievements will bring lasting happiness, only for reality to deliver a fleeting buzz followed by a return to baseline.

In his book *Stumbling on Happiness*, Harvard psychologist Daniel Gilbert explains this phenomenon beautifully. He found that we are terrible at predicting what will make us happy in the long run. We think that having all of our life's expectations met will bring lasting satisfaction but, instead, if these are met, we quickly adjust our benchmark for happiness and start chasing the next expectation.

And to make things even more convoluted and complex, we don't just have one expectation at a time. We have hundreds of expectations running around in our head. While we're conscious of some of these, mostly they're bubbling away in our subconscious—free from our critical assessment. We expect our partner to know what we're thinking. We expect traffic to be light or even non-existent whenever we need to drive somewhere. We expect our bodies to function perfectly every day, even as we get older. And when these expectations aren't met, frustration builds.

The worst part is expectations even undermine genuinely good moments. Think about a time when someone surprised you with kindness. Perhaps it was a stranger paying for your coffee or a friend sending an unexpected message of support because they know you've been stressed at work lately. You weren't expecting it, so it felt wonderful. What a pleasant and lovely surprise. Now contrast that with a time when you expected something—perhaps a birthday message from the same friend, or a raise at work for all the hard work you've been putting in. But you didn't get it. Even though nothing was technically taken away from you, this likely still felt like a loss. Finally, think of a time when you expected something to happen and it did. You got the raise that you felt you deserved or your friend called you for your birthday—as you expected that they would and should. How'd you feel? At best, you likely experienced a slight and temporary boost in happiness; at worst, you may have felt remarkably neutral about it. You expected it, and it happened—big whoop.

See how the two scenarios involving expectations either get us to net zero or, even worse, to disappointment? On the other hand, the scenarios free of expectations can create space and opportunity for happiness.

So when so many expectations can undermine your happiness and breed disappointment, what is the solution? I'm glad you asked. The answer is one word: appreciation.

If expectation is the thief of joy, appreciation is the security system that keeps it from being stolen.

At its core, appreciation is about shifting focus. Instead of dwelling on what should have happened, it invites you to engage with what is. Instead of focusing on the perfect reality that you imagine in your mind, you can instead interact with reality as it is. It's a subtle but profound mental reframe. Appreciation keeps you present. Instead of lamenting unmet expectations, you learn to embrace what is, even if it's imperfect.

Now, before I go any further, I want to address the elephant in the room: this is hard. If you've spent years (or decades) operating from a place of expectations, flipping the switch to appreciation won't happen overnight. It's a practice and a skill. And like all skills, it requires consistency.

Turning expectation into appreciation by letting go

The next time you find yourself frustrated, ask, 'What was I expecting?' Identifying the expectation is the first step. The next step is to pivot. Instead of dwelling on what didn't happen, look for something, anything, you can appreciate about the moment.

For example:

- *Expectation:* 'I expected my partner to notice I was upset and ask what's wrong.'
- *Reality:* They didn't.
- *Reframe:* 'I appreciate that even though they didn't notice, they consistently show love in other ways.'

Or:

- *Expectation:* 'I expected to get the job after a great interview.'
- *Reality:* The rejection email landed in your inbox.
- *Reframe:* 'I appreciate that I put myself out there, and I trust that another opportunity is on its way.'

This doesn't mean ignoring disappointment or pretending things don't hurt. It means acknowledging both. 'Yes, I'm disappointed and, yes, I can still find something to appreciate.' You can always find the silver linings to storm clouds, and the little moments of good in challenging chapters. And the more you practise finding them, the more automatic it becomes.

When expectations are left unchecked, they quietly erode your happiness. Appreciation, on the other hand, is an active choice. This choice brings you back to the present, shifts your focus to what's good, and makes life just a little bit lighter.

And if all else fails, remember this: happiness doesn't come from abandoning your goals, desires, hopes and standards alongside your expectations. This will only lead to apathy. Happiness comes from learning to hold your expectations, goals, desires, hopes and standards lightly enough that you can still appreciate life, even when it doesn't go to plan—and even when your expectations aren't met.

Reflection and application

Every time you feel irritated, disappointed or frustrated over the next week, pause and ask yourself:

- 'What expectation did I have?'
- 'Was it realistic or fair?'
- 'How can I shift my focus from expectation to appreciation?'

Write down your answers. Journaling this process makes it real. Over time, you'll start catching expectations before they lead to frustration. You'll start noticing patterns and areas where you routinely expect things to go a certain way. And once you see them, you can start to choose a different response.

Rewiring perspective: The art of seeing clearly

You may have heard the old fable about a farmer whose horse ran away. His neighbour, hearing the news, shook his head and said, 'Oh, what terrible luck'.

The farmer simply shrugged and replied, 'Maybe'.

A few days later, the horse returned, bringing with it three wild horses. The neighbour, wide-eyed with excitement, exclaimed, 'How wonderful!'

Again, the farmer shrugged. 'Maybe.'

The next day, the farmer's son tried to ride one of the wild horses, got thrown off and broke his leg. The neighbour, grim-faced, said, 'Oh no, what bad fortune'.

The farmer remained unfazed. 'Maybe.'

Soon after, the army came through the village, conscripting all the young men to fight in a war. But because of his broken leg, the farmer's son was spared. The neighbour, astonished, said, 'What incredible luck!'

The farmer, as you've probably guessed, said, 'Maybe'.

This story, often attributed to ancient Chinese philosophy, is one of the simplest and most profound illustrations of perspective I've found. We tend to label events as 'good' or 'bad' based on our immediate emotional response, but the truth is we don't always see the full picture. Something that seems disastrous in the moment could turn out to be a hidden blessing. Something we think is the best thing that's ever happened to us could have consequences we don't yet understand.

The lesson? Life rarely fits into neat categories of good and bad—it's all about how we choose to look at it. As Shakespeare noted in *Hamlet*, 'There is no good or bad but thinking makes it so'.

Before I dive into how to train your mind to take a more balanced perspective, let's talk about why we're so bad at it in the first place.

Remember back at the start of this chapter when I mentioned our brain's negativity bias? That same wiring is also responsible for worst-case-scenario thinking. Remember: our brains evolved to keep us safe, not happy. In prehistoric times, assuming the worst—'That rustling in the bushes is probably a tiger'—was a survival mechanism. The humans who took risks and saw the world through rose-coloured glasses? Many of them didn't live long enough to pass on their genes. That's right, the natural-born optimists died out generations ago.

Fast-forward to today and our brain is still running that same outdated software. Only now, instead of worrying about tigers, we catastrophise about emails left unanswered, text messages without replies and whether that offhanded comment we made on a date has permanently tanked our chances of a relationship.

The good news is we can change this.

Looking at the worst case, best case and most likely case

The third tool in your brain retraining toolkit is a simple but transformative exercise: worst-case, best-case and most likely case thinking. Here's how it works. Let's say you have a big presentation at work tomorrow, and you're spiralling into stress. Your mind is feeding you a horror story: What if I stumble over my words? What if I forget everything? What if my boss secretly hates me and this is my one shot to prove my worth? This is worst-case-scenario thinking in action.

Step one in retraining your brain is to lean into it fully. Let your brain go all the way to worst-case-scenario town. What's the absolute worst thing that could happen? Maybe you blank out completely. Maybe someone laughs. Maybe you get fired, end up bankrupt and have to move back in with your parents. Dramatic? Yes. But our brains are dramatic. Getting your worst-case scenario down on paper helps you see just how absurd your fear often is.

Next, flip it on its head. What's the absolute best possible outcome? If you could dream up the rosiest possible outcome for how things would play out, what would that be? Maybe you give the best presentation of your life, your boss is so impressed that they fast-track your promotion and you're celebrated in the company newsletter as a rising star.

Now you've got two extremes. One is fuelled by fear, while the other is fuelled by unfiltered optimism.

Finally, find the middle ground. Life is very rarely as good or as bad as our minds like to believe it could be. Your brain plays in the extremes and in black and white, whereas reality exists in the messy middle—in the shades of grey. So now ask yourself, 'What's the most likely scenario?' Chances are, you'll stumble over a word or two in your presentation, but no-one will really notice. Your boss will nod along, offer a few comments and life will go on. It won't be the defining moment of your career, good or bad.

By consciously walking through these three perspectives, you pull yourself out of catastrophising and into clarity. Instead of letting your brain go to worst-case scenario first—and then pitch a tent and stay there—you expand your perspective to something that's likely a lot more accurate.

Looking at what's in your control

You can expand the impact of this simple thought experiment by adding one final step to the process. After you've mapped out the worst-case, best-case and most likely scenarios, ask yourself, 'What's actually in my control?' This question is a game-changer. It shifts the focus from anxiety to action. Because while you can't control every outcome, you can influence how things unfold. You might be able to shift the most likely scenario to be a little closer to the best-case scenario with a couple of strategic actions.

Using our presentation example:

- You can't control your boss's reaction, but you could rehearse your key points so you feel more confident about what you're presenting.
- You can't guarantee you won't feel nervous, but you can take a few deep breaths beforehand to calm your body.
- You can't make people pay attention, but you can structure your talk in a way that's engaging. You could include more stories, for example, or vary your pitch so it's not a monotone monologue that drifts people off to sleep.

Focusing on what's in your control gives your brain something productive to do instead of spiralling into fear. It replaces helplessness with agency.

This approach isn't just useful for big moments like major work presentations, but also applies to a bunch of day-to-day challenges that often chip away at our happiness.

Stuck in traffic and worried about being late? Run through the various scenarios:

- *Worst case:* Your boss is annoyed.
- *Best case:* You arrive just in time.
- *Most likely:* You get there a little late, apologise and move on.
- *What's in your control?* You can't change the traffic, but you can call ahead and give a heads-up.

Or perhaps you're arguing with your partner and feeling like your relationship is doomed:

- *Worst case:* You break up.
- *Best case:* You resolve things and grow stronger.
- *Most likely:* You work through it, because no relationship is perfect.
- *What's in your control?* You can listen more, communicate better and take responsibility for your part.

By zooming out in this way, you remind yourself that most things aren't as bad, or as perfect, as your mind makes them out to be.

The more you practise expanding your perspective, the faster your brain will learn to do this automatically. And the best part is that, over time, you'll start to trust that no single event defines you. You'll start to believe that even when things don't go to plan, you have the resilience and resourcefulness to adapt. Because, at the end of the day, life is just like the farmer's story at the start of this section. What seems like a setback today could be setting you up for something better tomorrow.

So next time life throws you a curveball, instead of immediately labelling it as 'good' or 'bad', take a breath and remind yourself: 'maybe'.

Reflection and application

For the next week, whenever you find yourself anxious, overwhelmed or catastrophising, pause and go through this process:

1. *What's the worst-case scenario?* Write it down in vivid detail. Let your brain exaggerate if it wants to.
2. *What's the best-case scenario?* Flip it. What's the absolute best possible outcome?
3. *What's the most likely scenario?* Find the middle ground. What's the realistic outcome?
4. *What's in my control?* Identify two to three small actions you can take to influence the outcome in a positive way.

Do this in a journal, on your phone or even just in your head. I kid you not, one of our members at BU Happiness College would run through this practice on her kitchen backsplash with a whiteboard marker. She would get home from work and practise it while cooking dinner — genius, in my opinion.

Retraining your brain: A work in progress

As we end this chapter, I hope you've learned that your brain, when left to its own devices, can be a bit of a drama queen. It fixates on the negative, sets expectations that reality often fails to meet and builds castles out of worst-case scenarios. But, hopefully you've also learned that, with practice, you can retrain your brain. You can shift from dwelling in problems to noticing the good, from rigid expectations to flexible appreciation, and from anxious worst-case-scenario thinking to forming a more balanced and grounded perspective of life.

That's not a small thing. In fact, it's one of the five most powerful skills you can develop for your happiness (hence, its inclusion in this book). But, as I keep harping on and on about in nearly every chapter, you're not supposed to get this perfect.

If you walk away from this chapter thinking anything along the lines of, *Great, I'm going to practise gratitude every day, never let expectations ruin my mood and always reframe my perspective in a healthy way!*, then I hate to break it to you, but you've kind of missed the point. Remember—the goal here isn't perfection. The goal is progress.

That's why I gave you three different approaches to experiment with when it comes to retraining your brain: gratitude, expectation management and perspective shifting. To put it simply, no single tool works for everyone in every situation. Maybe you'll fall in love with gratitude and make it a daily ritual. Maybe expectation management will be your lightbulb moment. Maybe perspective shifting will be the thing that stops your spiralling thoughts in their tracks. Or maybe all three will work for you but at different times and in different ways.

This is an experiment, not a test you need to ace. Try each tool. Play with them. See what fits. And don't panic if one of them doesn't click immediately. That doesn't mean you're doing it wrong. It just means you're human.

And speaking of being human, give yourself time. Your brain has been running its current patterns for years and possibly decades. You didn't develop these mental habits overnight, and you're not going to rewire them overnight either. But with consistency, patience and self-compassion, you will notice a shift. You'll perhaps feel a little more ease and a little less stress. You'll notice a growing ability to catch yourself before the spiral, to shake off the weight of impossible expectations, and to actually notice and savour the good in your life. And, in my humble opinion, that's worth the work.

So, take a breath. Take your time. Try things out. Keep what works. Let go of what doesn't. And, most importantly, keep showing up for yourself. Because the more you do, the more you'll start to see that your brain is trainable. And when you train it to work *with* your happiness instead of *against* it, life starts to feel a whole lot better.

Chapter 5

Knowing yourself

The fourth skill of happiness

I still remember the exact moment that the importance and values of this fourth happiness skill hit me. Not in a gentle, 'Oh, that's interesting' kind of way, but in a 'someone just pulled the rug out from under me' kind of way.

I was sitting across from one of my earliest mentors, eager to soak up his wisdom on happiness, self-worth and confidence. I had my little checklist of things I wanted to work on, ready to go. 'I want to be more self-confident', I told him. 'I want to be kinder to myself. I want to stop being so critical. I want to take better care of myself. I want to be more self-compassionate. I want to build more self-trust.'

He nodded, jotting down notes as I spoke, and when I finished, he read them back to me. 'Self-confidence. Self-compassion. Self-care. Self-trust. Self-worth.'

In an attempt to frantically cover up my own emotional vulnerability, I replied in jest, 'Yep, that's it. I'll take three scoops of each of them please'.

He paused and then asked me a question that fundamentally changed the way I viewed personal growth. 'What do all of these things have in common?'

I frowned, unsure where he was going with this. 'Uh, they all start with "self"?'

'Exactly', he said, setting his pen down. 'So tell me—who is Declan?'

I opened my mouth, but no words came out. I had nothing. I could talk about my job, my achievements, my relationships and my hobbies, but who I was? What I stood for? What I truly valued? I had no idea.

And that's when he hit me with the real kicker. 'You're trying to build a healthy relationship with someone you don't even know yet.'

Ouch. But he was right. How could I expect to have self-worth when I hadn't defined what made me *me*? How could I cultivate self-trust when I didn't even understand my own guiding principles? How could I practice self-care when I had no idea what truly nourished me? Self-care, self-trust, self-esteem, self-worth, self-confidence and self-compassion all started with knowing myself.

That conversation left a mark on me, one I carry to this day. It provided a lesson I hope to now pass on to you.

Doing the work of knowing yourself

If you want to be happier, if you want to feel more grounded, confident and aligned in your life, you have to do the work of knowing yourself—and not just in a vague, 'I kind of know what I like' way, but in a deep, intentional way. You need to get to know yourself to the level where you can clearly articulate your values, strengths and what truly matters to you.

Because here's the truth: you can't have a strong, fulfilling relationship with someone you don't understand, and that includes yourself. Put down plainly like this likely sounds obvious, but most people never take the time to ask themselves, 'Who am I, really?' Instead, we slip into something easier—we become who we think we're supposed to be in order to appeal to the expectations of others.

That's the real danger of not defining yourself. You don't just float through life in a comfortable haze of indecision. You actively become a version of yourself that is shaped by external expectations. You become a human chameleon, constantly adjusting your colours to fit whatever environment you find yourself in. You try to be the perfect employee, the perfect partner, the perfect friend and the perfect parent. You shape-shift, tweak and edit yourself to meet the demands of different people, different roles and different situations. And, in doing so, you lose track of yourself entirely.

According to palliative care nurse Bronnie Ware, the single most common regret people have on their deathbeds is, 'I wish I'd had the courage to live a life true to myself, not the life others expected of me'.

Sit with that for a second.

This isn't a small regret, like wishing they'd travelled more or learned to play an instrument. This is the kind of regret that gnaws at the very core of a person. It's a profoundly troubling realisation that they spent decades being who they thought they should be, instead of who they truly were. It's the realisation that they had outsourced their identity to their family, their workplace, their culture and their social circles. They realise they traded pieces of themselves for approval, belonging or a false sense of security.

And the worst part? They didn't realise this until it was too late.

That's what happens when you don't take the time to define yourself. You don't necessarily feel lost. Indeed, it's perfectly possible, even likely, that you can live a busy, productive, even accomplished life without getting to know yourself on a deeper level. But an emptiness lurks underneath it, and a gnawing sense that something isn't quite right. And that could be because you've built your entire sense of self around what you do instead of building it around who you are.

But it doesn't have to be this way. Knowing yourself is one of the most profound gifts you can give yourself. When you have a deep understanding of your values, your strengths and what truly matters to you, everything else becomes easier. Decision-making becomes clearer. Confidence comes more naturally. You stop second-guessing yourself because you're no longer looking for external validation to confirm your decisions. You make the right choices because you already know what aligns with you.

This chapter, about the happiness skill of knowing yourself, sits at the heart of this book for a reason. I believe this is the most important skill you'll learn here—which is also why this is one of the longer chapters in the book. This skill is even more important than expanding your emotional intelligence, looking inward or even retraining your brain. Because at the end of your life, when you're looking back on the time you had, your happiness won't be defined simply by how you felt. It will be determined by how you lived. And how you live is inevitably shaped by who you are. It's shaped by your identity and sense of self.

It's no coincidence that I named the social enterprise I run BU Happiness College. People often ask me, 'What does the BU stand for?' The answer is in the name itself: BU. Be you.

I believe the greatest gift we can give ourselves, our loved ones and the world as a whole is to do the work of deeply understanding who we are. We need to define ourselves, not based on what others expect but on our own values and strengths. We need to form a healthy, trusting relationship with ourselves and live life on our terms, not someone else's.

This isn't just a trope of modern self-help; instead, it is wisdom that has echoed through the ages. 'Know thyself' was inscribed (in Greek) on the Temple of Apollo in Delphi, an ancient reminder that true wisdom begins within. The philosopher Lao Tzu put it simply in chapter 33 of his seminal work, *Tao Te Ching*: 'He who knows others is wise. He who knows himself is enlightened'.

And then there's the modern proverb (often misattributed to Oscar Wilde), 'Be yourself; everyone else is already taken'. While the original source may be unclear, the sentiment remains. The world doesn't need you to be a carbon copy of someone else. It needs you—your unique strengths, your voice and your perspective.

You've already laid the groundwork with the preceding three skills. You've learned how to work with your emotions rather than against them. You've developed introspection. You've started retraining your brain to focus on the good. These are the tools that allow you to sit with yourself without judgement, and to explore who you truly are without getting lost in negative spirals or external expectations. Because trying to figure out who you are while your mind is cluttered with doubt, negativity and everyone else's opinions is a losing battle. And that's exactly why we're going to do this together.

If I just asked you right now, 'Who are you?', you'd probably feel the same way I did in that coaching session—like you're staring at a blank canvas, unsure where to even begin. So instead of expecting you to pull a fully formed definition of yourself out of thin air, I'm going to help you approach this more like a paint-by-numbers exercise.

In the following section, I break this skill down into three core areas and tools:

1. *Your core values:* These are the non-negotiable principles that guide your decisions and shape your sense of integrity.
2. *Your character strengths:* These are the natural abilities and traits that make you uniquely you.
3. *Your love languages:* This is how you express and receive love, both in relationships and in your relationship with yourself.

By the end of this chapter, you'll have a much clearer picture of who you are, what matters to you and how to align your life with that knowledge. And once you do, all of the other skills of happiness will become easier to learn, practice and uphold. Decisions become clearer. Boundaries become stronger. Confidence becomes more natural. You can start living more authentically and wholeheartedly, because you have the tools, the clarity and the inner wisdom to be you.

Uncovering and living your core values

Picture this. You're standing at a crossroads in your career—a conundrum that billions of people before you have faced. In this particular case, one of the career paths ahead of you potentially leads to financial success and stability, but it demands long hours and sacrifices that leave little time for relationships or passion projects. The other path offers deep personal fulfilment and creative freedom but comes with uncertainty and financial risk.

Which do you choose? And why?

Or imagine this. You're in a heated argument with your partner, not over anything that will make or break your relationship, but more a trivial disagreement. One part of you wants to prove their point. In that moment, justice, fairness, standing your ground and maybe even being right all feel important. But another part of you is craving connection and harmony, and you know that pushing harder will only widen the gap between you. How do you decide what to do? And how do you decide in a moment when your emotions are heightened and your judgement is clouded?

What about something even simpler? It's Friday night and you're exhausted. Your week has been filled with curveballs and problems, and the weekend ahead is already jam-packed with social commitments. You've been looking forward to a quiet evening to yourself, but at 6 pm your best friend sends you an unexpected invitation to come out for dinner. You know that your friend has been going through a tough time recently, and that they rarely reach out to ask for help or someone to talk to. Do you push through and show up for your friend, or do you honour your need for rest?

These questions don't have perfectly right or wrong answers. You can't pass or fail at them. But if you struggled to answer them, if you hesitated or felt pulled in different directions, chances are you're not entirely clear on what your values are. And if you're not clear on your values, making decisions—big or small—can feel like stumbling through life without a map.

Your values act as your internal compass. They influence the choices you make, the way you react to situations and even the relationships you build. When you're clear on your values, you don't waste time agonising over decisions. You simply hold them up to the light of what truly matters to you, and the best path forward reveals itself.

But here's the problem: most of us never take the time to uncover our values. Instead, we drift through life adopting the values that society, our families or our workplaces expect of us. We absorb these values without questioning them. We chase things we think should make us happy, such as status, wealth and approval. And we don't stop to ask, 'Is this actually aligned with who I am? Do I even care about these things?'

No wonder so many people feel stuck or lost. They're following a script that wasn't written for them in the first place. They're living by inherited values they've absorbed from parents, teachers, friends and culture. And when we live by values that aren't truly ours, we feel a sense of unease. We might follow the 'right' path of getting the degree, climbing the corporate ladder, settling into the relationship that looks good on paper, but something feels off. We're ticking all the boxes but wondering why we still feel disconnected. Why we don't feel happy.

So, let's fix that.

The concept of values has been around for as long as human beings have been trying to make sense of their place in the world. Ancient philosophers spoke about living a virtuous life, religions framed values as sacred principles and, in more recent years, psychology has backed up what humans have always intuitively known: when we live in alignment with our values, we feel happier, more fulfilled and more resilient in the face of life's challenges. Studies show that people who live in alignment with their core values experience higher levels of wellbeing, greater resilience and deeper life satisfaction. Why? Because when you honour your values, you feel like you're living authentically—and authenticity is a powerful predictor of happiness.

This section is all about uncovering your true values, the ones that resonate at your core, not the ones you think you should have. Once you know your true values, everything else—such as your goals, your decisions and your happiness—starts falling into place.

This brings me to a critical question…

Are you living your values or someone else's?

Here's where a lot of people get stuck. They confuse socially expected values with their true values. Ask a room full of people to list their top five values, for example, and I guarantee you'll see the same words popping up again and again—family, integrity, kindness, creativity and success. But if you take a closer look at people's actions and the choices that they make, those values don't seem to hold up. Maybe someone claims that family is their top value, but they rarely make time for their loved ones. Maybe they say they value creativity, but they haven't engaged in a creative pursuit in years. Or maybe society has conditioned them to value financial success above all else. So they pursue a high-paying career, only to realise years later that what they really crave is meaningful work and human connection.

I'm not judging anyone here. However, this mismatch could be a sign that the values you first think of might not actually be your own. They're likely the values you think you should have, not necessarily the ones that are truly driving you as an individual.

This is why uncovering your values requires honesty. You have to separate *should* values from *true* values. The easiest way to do this is to look at your life:

- Where do you spend your time, energy and money?
- What moments in your life have felt the most fulfilling?

If your so-called value doesn't show up in your actions, chances are it's an inherited or socially expected value rather than a core one.

And this brings me to another important distinction to make…

Core values versus contextual values

Some values run deep, showing up in every area of your life. They're present in how you work, how you love and how you spend your time. These are your core values. They're the unshakable principles that define who you are at your best.

Other values are more situational. Perhaps you deem them as crucially important in some areas of your life, but not all that applicable to other areas of your life. These are contextual values.

Both core values and contextual values have their place and their purpose. Thinking of your unique collection of values as being like a tree can be helpful here. Your core values are the trunk. They're stable, strong and ever-present. They hold you up and form the heart of who you are as a person. Your contextual values are the branches, extending into different areas of your life. You might have a branch that you label 'career', one called 'relationships', another named 'health' and one dedicated to your 'personal growth'. The values that sit on each of these branches are a big part of how you make decisions related to that specific branch, but may not be considered when making decisions related to another branch of your life.

For example, someone might have 'freedom' as a core value. As such, it shows up everywhere in their life, including in how they structure their career (choosing flexibility over a rigid corporate job), how they travel (preferring spontaneous adventures over packaged tours), and even how they manage relationships (valuing autonomy and independence).

Meanwhile, they might have a contextual value of ambition in their work life but not in their personal life. They want to excel professionally, but when it comes to friendships and hobbies, they have no interest in competition or pursuing larger goals and achievements.

This distinction matters. Many people assume they have conflicting values but, often, it's just a case of not recognising where those specific values apply within their life. In the following figure, I've shared a simplified version of my personal values tree (overleaf) as an example to help you create your own. Note that in this example, I've only listed three areas of life with their associated contextual values. The full version of my values tree is a little larger, with up to seven distinct branches that change based on what areas of life are most important to me at that given time.

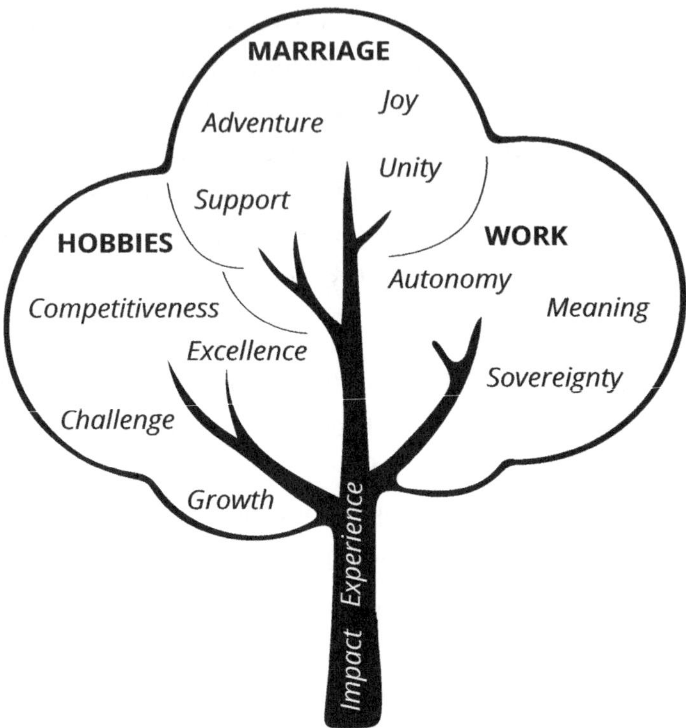

My example personal values tree

Living in alignment with your values

Knowing your values is just the beginning. The real work is aligning your decisions, behaviours and relationships with these values. A simple practice to start doing this is to use your values as a decision-making filter. Before saying yes or no to something, ask, 'Does this align with my core values?' For example:

- If you value freedom, does saying yes to that rigid job contract make sense?
- If you value connection, are you prioritising meaningful relationships in your daily life?

- If someone watched a replay of your life over the past few months, would they be able to see your values in action and in practice?

If you take one thing away from this section of the book, let it be this: living in alignment with your values will make you happier than any external achievement ever will.

Your values are your compass. Use them, trust them and, most importantly, live them. At the end of your life, your greatest success won't be found in meeting society's expectations. It will be found in living a life that felt deeply true to yourself.

Reflection and application

No one-size-fits-all approach is best when trying to discover your values, so I'm going to give you a few different approaches here. Pick the one that resonates most with you. And remember — the goal isn't to choose the 'right' values. It's to choose your values.

The 'what's this value in service of?' test

Sometimes what you think is a core value is actually just a stepping stone to something deeper. Ask yourself, 'What is this value in service of?'

For example, I used to think my core value was growth. But when I kept asking what growth was in service of for me, I realised it was all about impact. My core value was really about helping others, creating positive change and making a difference — and growth was always the means to that end. In other words, 'growth' was a method, but 'impact' was the goal.

(continued)

The values list approach

Take a list of common values (many options are available online). Circle any that resonate. Don't overthink it. Just go with what instinctively feels important. You'll likely end up with 20 or 30. Now, start eliminating. Group similar ones together. Ask yourself, 'If I could only keep one of these, which would it be?' Repeat this process until you're left with three to five values that feel truly essential.

The peak experience method

Reflect on three to five moments in your life when you felt the most alive, fulfilled or at peace. What was present in those moments? What do they have in common? The underlying themes will point to your values.

To solidify and stress-test your values, take the list of values you've created and ask yourself these five questions:

1. 'Does this value show up consistently in my life?'
2. 'Is this value in service of something deeper, or is it valuable in and of itself?'
3. 'How can I remind myself of this value on a day-to-day basis?'
4. 'What behaviours and habits do I currently have that uphold this value?'
5. 'What behaviours and habits do I currently have that are in conflict with this value?'

Discovering and using your character strengths

Long before self-help became an aisle in the bookstore, psychology had a problem. For most of its early history, it was a field obsessed with what could go wrong with the human mind. Depression, anxiety, trauma, addiction—if it was perceived or labelled as being 'broken', psychology wanted to study it and try to 'fix' it. Don't get me wrong, that work was (and still is) incredibly important. But it created a kind of lopsidedness. We developed an encyclopaedia of diagnoses (the *Diagnostic and Statistical Manual of Mental Disorders*, or *DSM*), filled with all the things that could go 'wrong' with the human psyche. But we had no equivalent for what could go right.

That changed in the early 2000s when Dr Martin Seligman, one of the founding figures of positive psychology, asked a simple but profound question: what if we studied what's right with people instead of what's wrong? What if we created a framework that focused not on dysfunction but on strengths? And what if we magnified the traits that help people thrive?

In chapter 1, I outlined the PERMAH model of happiness and highlighted that this model was based on the work of Dr Seligman. Well, the PERMAH model isn't the only great contribution that positive psychology has made to our understanding of human happiness. I believe another framework is even more valuable, especially when it comes to the happiness skill of deeply knowing yourself.

Enter the Values in Action (VIA) Survey of Character Strengths. This framework, developed by Dr Seligman and Dr Christopher Peterson, identified 24 universal strengths that exist across cultures, ages and backgrounds. As shown in the following table (overleaf), the list includes kindness, creativity, perseverance, humour and love of learning—strengths of the head and the heart. Seligman and Peterson found that knowing and using your own character strengths is strongly linked to increased happiness, fulfilment, confidence and even better interpersonal outcomes such as healthier and happier marriages.

The 24 VIA Character Strengths

Appreciation of beauty and excellence	Bravery	Creativity
Curiosity	Fairness	Forgiveness
Gratitude	Honesty	Hope
Humility	Humour	Judgement
Kindness	Leadership	Love
Love of learning	Perseverance	Perspective
Prudence	Self-regulation	Social intelligence
Spirituality	Teamwork	Zest

This approach is especially refreshing in a world where most self-help is still quietly built on shame. Think about it. So many self-improvement books really just outline what the author says is 'wrong' with you and how they recommend you go about 'fixing' it. You need to be more confident. You need to be more disciplined. You need to wake up earlier, hustle harder, earn more, meditate longer and have a morning routine so perfect it makes Olympic athletes feel lazy.

Modern self-help often convinces us that we need to be everything to everyone. It whispers the message that we are not enough, and that to be happy, we have to constantly work on our weaknesses. But here's the truth: no one is great at everything. And trying to be is a fast track to burnout and self-doubt. That's the trap modern self-help sets for us. All too often, it sells us the idea that we're always falling short, that we'll finally be worthy once we 'fix' all the broken parts.

Focusing on your character strengths flips that script. This approach says, 'Hey, you're already good at something. Start there'. By using your strengths more often, especially your signature strengths (your top five), you feel more energised, more capable and more you. You perform better at work, you build deeper connections in your relationships and you bounce back faster from setbacks. Why? Because you're operating from a place of authenticity. You're not trying to be someone else. You're showing up as your best self more consistently.

That's what makes this tool so powerful, and why I'm so excited to share it with you. And the good news is discovering your strengths doesn't have to be a guessing game. Thanks to the VIA Institute on Character, you can take a completely free, research-backed assessment online that ranks your 24 strengths from most naturally occurring to least. I encourage you to take the assessment if you haven't already (and I've provided information on how to do so in the 'Reflection and application' box at the end of this section).

But before I get too carried away by my own enthusiasm, let's pause here for a moment and clarify a few things.

Character strengths are different from values

Character strengths aren't the same as values, although the two are often confused. Values are what matter to you. They're your guiding principles. Strengths, on the other hand, are how you naturally think, feel and behave when you're at your best. They're the traits that energise you and the things that you're uniquely good at. So, while your values might lead you to care deeply about justice, your strengths might show up in how you pursue that value. You could pursue the value of justice, for example, through the strengths of bravery, leadership or social intelligence.

Focus on strengths, not weakness

Once you take the test, and before you start redesigning your life, a quick warning: it's very human to look at your top five strengths with curiosity and then immediately scroll to the bottom and think, *Oh no. I'm terrible at self-regulation. Better fix that immediately.*

But remember that's not the goal here. The goal is not to treat the bottom of your character strengths list as a collection of weaknesses that you must correct. It's to understand that those are just traits that aren't as naturally energising or prominent for you. You still have access to all 24 of the character strengths and you're capable of practising any of them, but whether through nature or nurture your top five strengths will come to you a little more naturally than the others. That's why we call them your 'signature' strengths. These are the ones I encourage you to focus on. They're the ones that allow you to bring your best self to the table. Whether when you're at work, in your relationships or during moments of personal challenge, these strengths are your secret sauce.

The goal isn't perfection but presence. Start small. Start where you are. And watch what happens when you begin to live not from a place of deficiency, but from a place of strength. Because being your best self doesn't require you to be great at everything. It just asks you to know what you're already great at and to use that as your foundation. You don't have to fix all your flaws to be worthy of happiness. You just need to bring more of you to the table.

Again, this doesn't mean ignoring your weaknesses. But it does mean flipping the focus. Instead of obsessing over what's 'wrong' with you, start paying more attention to what's already right. Instead of forcing yourself to slog through situations that drain you, look for ways to design your life around the activities and environments where your strengths shine.

This might sound like a luxury, but it's not. It's a responsibility. The world doesn't benefit from you being mediocre at everything. It benefits from you being brilliant at being you. And your signature strengths are the invitation to do exactly that.

Use your strengths daily

In a 2005 study, Dr Seligman, along with Tracy Steen, Nansook Park and Dr Peterson, found that participants who identified their signature strengths and used them in a variety of ways each day experienced lasting increases in happiness and decreases in depressive symptoms. Even more notably, they found that these effects held relatively steady even six months later. That's a pretty compelling return on investment for something that takes just a few minutes of awareness and intention each day.

Other studies have found that using your signature strengths regularly can lead to higher self-esteem, more frequent experiences of flow (the state of being completely immersed in what you're doing, explored in more detail in chapter 1), and better overall life satisfaction. In short, your strengths are a remarkably well-researched tool in your toolkit for a happier life.

So how do you use them? Let's look at a few examples.

Amanda, one of our members at BU Happiness College—to protect their privacy, all names here have been changed—discovered that one of her top strengths was curiosity. Before learning this, she often found herself feeling bored and disengaged at work. Meetings felt like groundhog day. Her projects felt uninspired. And her career was beginning to feel like it was stuck in a rut.

But once Amanda had the language to notice and describe her character strengths, something clicked. She realised she could bring curiosity into her daily work by asking better questions and exploring new ways of doing things. She even initiated 'learning lunches', where team members could share something interesting that they were exploring outside of their usual work roles. Not only did her energy for work come back, but her team also started to connect more deeply as well.

Then there was James, who was struggling in his relationship. He and his partner weren't fighting, but they weren't really connecting either. After doing the VIA strengths assessment, he found that appreciation of beauty and excellence was one of his signature strengths. At first, he brushed it off. 'What does that even mean?' he laughed. But we encouraged him to reflect on it.

He realised he often felt deeply moved by music, nature and moments of human kindness. But he rarely shared that side of himself with anyone else. So he started letting his partner in. They'd take walks and he'd point out the sunsets. He'd share songs that made him feel something. And he made a point of seeking out the beauty and excellence within his partner. Slowly but surely, they built a richer, more emotionally connected relationship. They didn't do this through grand gestures, but through small, meaningful moments that let James's true self shine through.

And these kinds of results are just as powerful in team environments.

My team and I at BU Happiness College have worked with sports teams and corporate groups of all sizes who've used strengths-based approaches to transform the way they operate. When each team member understands and articulates their unique strengths, and recognises the strengths of others, they move from competition to collaboration. They stop stepping on each other's toes trying to be the best at everything, and start complementing each other by bringing their best selves to the table. One team leader described it like this: 'It was like everyone stopped trying to be the same player and started playing their actual position. Suddenly we had flow'.

That's the magic of strengths. They allow you to contribute in a way that's energising, sustainable and true to who you are.

But as with any skill in this book, awareness isn't enough. You have to use your strengths. So, once you've taken the assessment and identified your top five, here's your challenge: choose one of them. Just one. And each day for the next week, find one small way to bring it into your life more intentionally. If humour is your strength, how can you bring lightness into your work day? If it's kindness, what's one act you could do, no matter how small, that lets that shine through?

Notice what happens when you use your strengths. Catch yourself in the act of using them. Then start bringing them into areas of your life where they're missing. Ask yourself:

- 'How can I use one of my top five strengths in a new way at work this week?'
- 'How can I use a strength in a relationship where I've been feeling disconnected?'
- 'How can I solve a current challenge using one of my strengths, instead of brute-forcing my way through it?'

And when life feels hard, as it inevitably will at times, let your strengths remind you that you've got more capacity than you think.

Reflection and application

Use the following steps to take advantage of your strengths:

1. Take the free VIA Strengths Survey at viacharacter.org.
2. Once you've received your results, write down your top five signature strengths.
3. Reflect on how each strength has shown up in your life recently. Where do you see it in action?
4. Choose one strength and brainstorm three new ways you could use it this week — in work, relationships or personal goals.
5. Share your top five strengths with a close friend, family member or partner. Ask them where they've seen those traits in you.
6. Keep a 'strengths journal' for a week: each day, write down one moment where you used a strength and what impact it had.
7. Recognise strengths in others. Whether it's your partner, colleague, friend or teammate, catch them using their strengths and call it out. Doing so deepens connection and helps them feel seen.

Embracing your love languages

Deeply knowing yourself is about more than just forming a better relationship with yourself. It is also an essential part of cultivating another human need that is essential for a fulfilling life: the need for love.

Love, after all, is at the heart of so many things we crave—meaningful connection, belonging, a sense of safety, warmth, and understanding. These are all underpinned by the human desire to love and to be loved. You might remember back in chapter 1 we explored the PERMAH model, the research-backed framework that underpins a life of thriving and happiness. And one of the most powerful, impactful and consistently researched ingredients in that model? Relationships.

We simply cannot flourish in isolation. Happiness, as I've said before, is not a solo pursuit. It is co-created—in conversations, in shared experiences, and in the ways we show up for others and let them show up for us. Yet, for all its importance, love and connection remain some of the most misunderstood and unpractised skills in modern life. Most people want better relationships. But very few are ever taught how to build them. And fewer still are ever taught how they can personally express and experience love in all its many forms.

We're told that love is something we just 'fall into'. We're made to believe closeness should be effortless, and that if it's hard work, something must be wrong. And yet... we struggle. We misread people. We feel misunderstood ourselves. We show love the way we want to receive it and are surprised when it doesn't land the way we intended. That's where this third tool comes in. It's time to look at how you give and receive one of the most powerful forces for happiness on the planet: love.

Now, when I say love, I also want to expand that definition beyond the 'hearts and roses' kind. More than one 'flavour' of love is possible, and ancient Greek philosophers knew this well. Indeed, they had distinct words to describe the different types:

- *Eros:* Romantic, passionate love.
- *Philia:* Deep friendship or brotherly love.
- *Storge:* Familial love like the bond between parent and child.

- *Agape:* Unconditional love, often associated with altruism.
- *Ludus:* Playful, flirtatious love.
- *Pragma:* Long-standing, practical love.
- *Philautia:* Love of self.
- *Mania:* Obsessive or possessive love.

Modern culture tends to zero in on eros and ignore the rest. But if you only focus on romantic love, you miss out on all the other ways love can show up in your life. You can experience a loving connection with your friends, colleagues, children, community and even with strangers. And all of it contributes to a happier, richer life.

So how do you better understand how you express and receive love in all its forms? One framework I've found useful is the five 'love languages', originally introduced by Dr Gary Chapman.

Now, I'll be upfront: this tool doesn't have the same level of scientific rigour or decades of validated psychological research behind it as the VIA Character Strengths or values work. It's not airtight. It's been critiqued. And that's fair. But I've still chosen to include it here because, despite its limitations, it continues to offer people something genuinely useful. And it does so through:

- prompting self-reflection
- giving us a language to better communicate our needs
- offering a simple, accessible framework to better understand ourselves and the people we care about.

And, honestly, in a world where many people struggle to ask for what they need or to understand why their relationships feel slightly 'off', that can be a game-changer.

That said, I'm not going to unpack this tool in as much depth as I did with values and character strengths. And that's intentional. A whole book is already dedicated to this (it's conveniently called

The Five Love Languages by Dr Gary Chapman) and if this section piques your interest, I'd strongly encourage you to explore it more deeply by reading that book.

My goal here is to simply introduce you to the concept, help you reflect on how it might show up in your life, and point you in the right direction if you want to take it further. And, perhaps most importantly, I want to expand your understanding of love beyond the romantic clichés we often default to.

Love, in all its forms, enriches our lives. And when we get better at giving and receiving it, when we bring intention and awareness to the ways we connect, we not only live more fulfilling lives ourselves but also ripple that fulfilment out to others.

So while this tool may not be as scientifically supported as the ones that came before, it still earns its place here. I'm not offering it as a definitive guide, but as a spark and a conversation starter. It could become a bridge between who you are and how you relate to the people around you.

The idea is simple. Different people give and receive love in different ways. Understanding your own preferences, as well as those of the people closest to you, can dramatically improve your relationships—not because you're trying harder, but because you're trying smarter.

The five love languages are:

1. *Words of affirmation:* You feel loved when someone expresses their love through words, including compliments, appreciation and encouragement.
2. *Acts of service:* You feel most loved when someone does something thoughtful for you, such as cooking a meal, helping with a task or easing a burden.

3. *Receiving gifts:* This language is not about materialism, but thoughtfulness. You feel loved when someone gives you something meaningful, no matter how small.
4. *Quality time:* You feel loved through undivided attention and shared experiences.
5. *Physical touch:* You feel loved through physical presence and contact, such as hugs, high-fives, a pat on the back or even a reassuring hand on the shoulder.

Importantly, your love language is also the way you express love. So if you feel love through words of affirmation, this is how you often express it, even if the person you're expressing these words to has a love language of acts of service.

We all have a mix of love languages, but most people have one or two that feel especially meaningful. When those are missing in the other person in the relationship, or when we're giving love in a way that doesn't match the other person's language, it's like speaking English to someone who only understands French. The intention might be there, but the message gets lost in translation.

This framework isn't just useful in romantic relationships. It can be applied to friendships, family dynamics and even the workplace (yes, really). I once worked with a client who realised that her teenage son wasn't feeling as connected to her. This wasn't because he was inherently distant, although you may be able to relate to the challenge of connecting with a teenager, but because she'd been expressing love in a way that didn't resonate with him. She had been showing her love and care through acts of service, such as making his bed and packing his lunch. But what he really needed was more quality time with her and to hear more words of encouragement. That insight opened a door for them to connect more intentionally.

Or take another BU graduate. She was a manager who always bought coffee for her team, thinking it was a thoughtful gesture. While it definitely is a thoughtful gesture, she found that it wasn't going very far in creating the connection she wanted. Eventually, through curiosity, she discovered that most of her team responded better to ten minutes of one-on-one time or a simple 'great job' at the end of the day. The more she learned about her team, the more she was able to show them that she cared in the ways that best made them feel cared about. Once she adapted her approach, her team morale and engagement skyrocketed.

As you can see, it's not necessarily about doing more. It's about doing differently. It's about being intentional with how you show people that you give a damn about them—and, in turn, how you recognise when other people give a damn about you. That's the magic of understanding love languages.

Of course, no tool is perfect. Some critics argue that the framework oversimplifies a complex concept. And that's fair. Love is complex. It's chaotic. It's messy. It's convoluted. It's multifaceted. And all of that is part of why it's so beautiful. But I'd argue that most of us aren't looking for more complexity in our lives. We're looking for small and simple ways to bring a sense of clarity to the complexity. We're looking for connection amid the chaos. And we're looking for direction through the messiness. And if this tool gives you a way to build that through starting a conversation, it's worth exploring.

So, how do you find your love language? You could take one of the countless free online quizzes that show up when you google 'love languages test'. Or you could simply reflect on the moments you've felt most appreciated or close to someone. What were they doing? What made you feel loved? What were you doing in return? These clues often point to your preferences.

The bigger takeaway here isn't to obsess over getting it 'right'. It's to begin a conversation with yourself and with the people around you. It's to become more intentional about how you give love and more aware of how you like to receive it.

Because in a world that often tells us to work harder, push more and do better as individuals, maybe the real happiness hack is this: love thoughtfully and love intentionally.

Reflection and application

Use the following to help find your love language, and that of those around you:

1. Take five minutes to reflect on the last time you felt truly appreciated or loved. What made that moment meaningful? Which love language does it reflect?
2. Identify the love languages you believe matter most to you. Which two stand out?
3. Have a conversation with someone close to you (your partner, friend, family member or colleague) about your love languages and ask about theirs.
4. Pick one relationship where you'd like to deepen connection. Try intentionally expressing love using the other person's preferred love language for one week.
5. If this topic interests you, dive deeper by reading *The Five Love Languages* by Dr Gary Chapman or exploring one of the online tools at 5lovelanguages.com.

Continuing your journey to yourself

By this point of the chapter (and the book), you've hopefully realised that getting to know yourself isn't about achieving some final version of you. It's about uncovering the traits that allow for a more honest, complete and fulfilling relationship with yourself.

This chapter hasn't given you a tidy set of labels to stick on your chest. It's given you tools—a starting point and a compass, not a map. What you do with those tools is entirely up to you. You might feel energised, scribbling down your values and identifying how they show up in your life. Or you might need time. You might take the VIA Character Strengths quiz and have an instant 'aha moment'. Or you might question it, reflect and tweak. You might feel uncertain about how to apply this or you might immediately feel a sense of direction click into place.

All of that is valid. This isn't a 'tick-the-box' exercise. Knowing yourself isn't something you knock over in a weekend workshop or a single journaling session. It's layered. It's seasonal. It shifts as you do. The man I am today is different to the man I was five years ago. As a result, some of my values, character strengths and love languages have shifted and evolved over time. I hope that I continue to grow, evolve and change as time goes on.

The work of getting to know yourself, truly, deeply and courageously, is not something you do once and tick off like a life admin task. It's not a clean-cut, single-answer quiz. It's a practice. It uncovers a relationship that is nurtured and upheld over time.

So here's the through-line: the more clearly you understand what matters to you, what you bring to the table and how you prefer to connect with others, the easier it becomes to live in a way that feels meaningful and authentic. You begin to feel as though you're living your life, not somebody else's life. And as you become clearer in knowing who you are, you will likely start making different decisions. You may start speaking up more when you used to stay quiet. Or perhaps you'll begin choosing rest when you used to push through. You might even get clearer on your boundaries. You could start saying no more often while feeling a little bit less guilty about it. You might even feel brave enough to start saying yes to bigger goals that scare and excite you, because you know they align with who you are.

You'll start building a life that doesn't just look good but also feels right—a life that feels like home. And that, ultimately, is the heart of this chapter. Not perfection or performance; just permission. This chapter is even an invitation:

- An invitation to stop outsourcing your identity to everyone else.
- An invitation to stop shape-shifting into what you think the world wants.
- An invitation to start coming home to who you already are.

And you're not doing so because it's trendy or profitable. And you're certainly not doing it because it's easy—after over a decade of doing this work, I can promise you that it won't be. I'm ending this chapter with this invitation solely because I believe that a fulfilling life can only be lived from the inside out. And that means, at some point, you need to stop looking 'out there' for answers, and start looking inside of yourself—in your head, in your heart and in your soul. These are the places where the truest expression of you has been all along.

Please remember this: the work of true happiness is not about fixing yourself. You were never broken. It's not about becoming someone else. It's about learning to be true to who you are.

Chapter 6

Directing your life

The fifth skill of happiness

Every journey, including the one we've taken together through this book, has a point when it's time to lift your gaze from the path in front of you and look up at the horizon. A time to take a breather on the mountain and set your sights to the summit; to stop making progress solely for the sake of making progress and start asking, 'Where am I going? What is all of this actually in service of?'

Because the truth is you can have all the happiness tools in the world—you can be emotionally intelligent, deeply self-aware, mentally clear and mindful—and still feel like you're drifting. Even when you master all of the happiness skills discussed so far, it's possible to still feel like you're stuck in the passenger seat of your own life.

Sometimes when I ask people how their life is going, they respond with something like, 'Oh, you know ... it's going'. And that's exactly it. For so many people, life doesn't feel lived—at least, not at its full potential. Life just kind of happens to them. They're busy, they're doing, they're achieving ... but somewhere along the way, they forgot to pause and ask if any of it is actually aligned with who they are and what they want from life. They're surviving, but they're not thriving.

This chapter is about changing that. It's about taking everything we've explored so far—your emotional intelligence, your ability to introspect, your retrained brain and your self-knowledge—and using it to build a future that matters and a future that feels distinctly yours.

In many ways, this chapter is the culmination of all the skills you've learned so far. Everything has been leading here. Because when you have the self-awareness to know who you are, and the emotional tools to stay present and grounded through life's inevitable turbulence, you become ready for the next great skill of happiness: directing your life with clarity and conviction. In other words, you become ready to live on purpose. This chapter is going to help you learn how to do exactly that.

Purpose versus vision and intention

Now, let me be clear up-front: when I say 'purpose', I don't mean you have to figure out some grand, noble mission to save the world. In fact, one of the first things I talk about in this chapter is the difference between all-caps *PURPOSE* (that big, daunting life's calling) and lowercase *purpose* (the daily sense of intention and meaning we bring to the way we live). The truth is both matter. And either one, when practised consistently, will deepen and enrich your experience of happiness.

I also talk about vision, that internal compass that points you toward a life that feels emotionally rich and right and true. Vision isn't about goals and checklists, but about crafting a bigger picture for the kind of life you want to live, the kind of person you want to be and the kind of impact you want to have. It's the 'why' behind the 'what'. And when you lose sight of your vision, you can easily fall into the trap of living a life that's busy but empty.

And, finally, I talk about intentionality, the daily art of living like you mean it. Because even if you've got the clearest vision and a deep sense of purpose, if you don't bring intention into how you show up, you risk letting life pull you in every direction but your own. You risk living a distracted life.

Let me offer you this image to explain this more fully. Imagine life is a road trip. Most people are just along for the ride. They're not picking the destination and they're not holding the map. Sometimes they're not even in the car. They're standing on the sidewalk, watching other people speed past and wondering why their own life feels stuck.

This chapter is about getting back in the car and getting behind the wheel. And, no, that doesn't mean you'll never hit a road bump again or you'll never get lost. What it means is that when the inevitable detours come (and they will), you'll have the capacity, clarity, confidence and internal compass to reroute. You'll know where you're heading and, perhaps even more importantly, you'll know why.

You may have come across the popular saying (commonly misattributed to Mark Twain), 'The two most important days in your life are the day you are born and the day you find out why'. While no credible evidence exists that Mark Twain ever wrote this sentence, my hope is that this chapter serves as a nudge toward that second day: the day you find out why you were born.

And don't worry. I'm not going to ask you to sit and meditate atop a mountain until a lightning bolt of clarity hits you. Nor am I going to tell you to fly to the Amazon to drink ayahuasca in the desperate hope that your life's purpose will be revealed to you in a drug-fuelled haze. Instead, I outline how purpose and direction are often discovered not through passive contemplation, but through action. They're discovered through trying things, reflecting on them and choosing what to care about.

By the end of this chapter, you won't have a rigid five-year plan. That's not the point. What you will have is a more compelling vision for your life, a clearer sense of the purpose you want to live by and a handful of practical tools to help you bring more intention into each day. You'll know how to define your own definition of a meaningful and fulfilling life, and how to start living it, one decision at a time.

Let's begin.

Vision: Defining your destination

GPS systems ask you to enter your destination before offering directions for a reason. No matter how well-equipped you are, no matter how fancy the car or how full the tank of petrol, if you don't know where you're going, all you're doing is moving. You're not progressing. You're just circling. And that's what life can feel like when you don't have a vision. You can be busy every hour of the day, productive to the point of exhaustion, checking off endless lists and still feel... adrift. You can feel like you're doing a lot but going nowhere that really matters—or worse, like you're climbing a ladder that's leaning up against the wrong wall.

That's where vision comes in. Vision gives your life direction. It gives your days depth. And it gives your efforts meaning. And, no, you don't have to create a perfectly polished, cinematic vision board with ethereal piano music playing in the background. Your vison doesn't need to be written up in calligraphy and framed on your office wall. It doesn't need to be captured in some Instagram-worthy collage that you upload with the caption #visionboard.

Of course, you can capture your vision through any of those approaches if you so choose. The only thing that really matters, however, is that your vision is yours. It shouldn't be a vision inherited from your parents, copied from social media or based on what other people think success should look like. Your vision is the internal compass that helps you live a life that feels aligned with you, not just the life you accidentally ended up in.

Think of vision as a lighthouse, not a prison. It's not a fixed destination that you're locked into. It's a glowing point on the horizon that keeps you oriented when the fog rolls in. And fog will roll in. We all have moments in life when we feel lost, stuck or unsure. That's part of being human. But having a clear vision is what helps you remember which direction to keep sailing in, even when the seas get rough and choppy.

Here's one thing I want to make really clear: your vision doesn't have to impress anyone. It doesn't have to win awards. It doesn't have to look like a script to a Hollywood biopic. It just has to be true. That might mean your vision is about building a business that changes the world. Or it might be about growing a garden, raising kind children, being a loyal friend, or simply living each day with peace and presence. There is no hierarchy here. No vision is too big or too small, as long as it feels meaningful to you.

One of the most practical journaling prompts you can use to get clearer on your vision is deceptively simple: 'What does a happy life look like to me?' Don't rush your answer to this question. Sit with it. Let it stretch. Your answer might come quickly, or it might trickle out in bits and pieces. You might even find your pen hovering over the page with no words coming at all. That's okay; you're not failing. You're just facing the blank page that most people avoid their whole lives.

We live in a world that tries to sell us a pre-packaged idea of happiness. We're told what we should want—a six-figure salary, perhaps, along with a house with a big backyard, and a certain body shape, job title, relationship status or social media following. But your vision isn't about what the world wants from you. It's about what your soul wants for you.

So if you feel like you're not quite sure what your vision is, welcome. That's a sign that you're actually paying attention. Remember that vision is less about having the answer and more about asking the right questions. Try some of the following:

- 'If my life could feel on purpose, what would it look like?'
- 'If nothing was off-limits, what kind of life would I love to wake up into?'
- 'At the end of my life, what would I want to be true about the way I lived?'

Let those questions simmer. Let them shake loose the inherited scripts, the old identities and the worn-out narratives that you've been carrying. And let them whisper something truer.

And remember: your vision doesn't have to be fully formed today. You're allowed to draft and redraft. You're allowed to change your mind. The version of you five years from now might have a slightly different vision for what a happy life entails. That's not a failure but a sign that you're evolving.

Typically what I witness among our members and graduates at BU Happiness College is that vision (your 'why') stays relatively stable over time. It may shift as you grow and change, but it's rare for it to change entirely. Goals, on the other hand (the methods to reach your vision), are more prone to change. Goals will shift as life unfolds while your vision acts as a steady anchor. Goals are the mile markers. Vision is the direction. Goals can be ticked off a list. Vision is something you live.

Here's a quick example of what this looks like in action. Imagine someone whose vision is to live a deeply creative life, surrounded by art, nature and meaningful relationships. That's their compass. Along the way, their goals might change. Maybe they become a painter, then a teacher, and then open a small studio space. None of those things are the vision; they're just different ways of living into it. If the studio closes or teaching no longer fits, the vision still holds. It's still their North Star.

So here's a reframe I want to offer you: don't stress if your vision feels broad or messy or uncertain at first. That's not only okay, but also expected. This isn't a branding exercise. It's an unfolding. And, sometimes, clarity comes slowly. That's why I'm not going to ask you to write a perfectly packaged 'life purpose statement' here. Instead, I'm inviting you to keep asking the questions that matter, to stay curious and to check in with yourself regularly. I'm asking you to keep orienting your life, one decision at a time, toward something that feels aligned and worthwhile.

And if you ever feel unsure, come back to this: does this decision, this path and this version of life feel like it's moving me closer to the person I want to be and the life I want to live? If yes, keep going. If no, adjust the wheel. Because you're not just here to survive the journey of life. You're here to direct it.

Reflection and application

Here's a short journaling exercise to help you define and refine your personal vision. You don't need to answer every question at once. Let this reflection be an ongoing conversation with yourself. Ask yourself:

- 'What does a happy and fulfilling life look like to me?'
- 'What does this life feel like?'
- 'If my life were a story, what would I want the central theme to be?'
- 'What kind of person do I want to become over the next five, ten, 20 years?'
- 'What kind of impact would I love to have — in my relationships, my community or the world?'
- 'What does "success" actually mean to me?'

Write freely. Revisit often. And don't worry about getting it perfect. Remember: your vision is not a verdict but a direction.

Purpose: What you show up for

If vision is your direction, the distant landscape you're steering toward, then purpose is what gets you out of bed and into the world each day. It's what pulls you forward when motivation wavers and the road gets rough. And unlike vision, which tends to stretch across the canvas of your entire life, purpose often lives in the smaller, more intimate brushstrokes. It's experienced in your daily actions and choices, and in the moments of life that feel deeply aligned to you.

But before I start unpacking the theory of purpose, let's pause for a second. Because 'purpose' is one of those words that can either inspire or intimidate. For many people, the moment they hear it, their brain flashes to something epic and unattainable—something like curing cancer, solving world hunger or launching the next billion-dollar company. Finding your 'purpose' sounds like a mountaintop that only the few and chosen get to climb. The rest of us? We're just here trying to pay the bills and remember where we put our keys.

But those epic ideas are not what living a purposeful life is about. At its core, purpose is simply about choosing what matters to you and showing up for it consistently. It's not about doing everything. It's about doing something that matters and that feels meaningful to you, even if it wouldn't make headlines. Sometimes that purpose is bold and blazing. Other times, it's quiet and steady. Sometimes it looks like starting a movement. Other times, it's making your child laugh after a hard day. Both matter. Both are purpose.

In fact, let's step away from the idea that purpose has to be found like some treasure buried deep in the jungle, revealed only to those with a machete and a penchant for philosophy. Here's what I now know to be true. Purpose isn't found. It's *created.* And it's created through our choices and actions, and through having the courage to show up, imperfectly and intentionally, for what we care deeply about.

Let's take that one step further. Because if one myth has tripped up more people than I can count, it's the commonly held idea that purpose will suddenly arrive in a flash of clarity, riding in on a lightning bolt moment of destiny. For years I chased this myth, thinking I'd suddenly find purpose like a crunched up $50 note in the pocket of my jeans. In reality? Purpose isn't something you discover by thinking harder or waiting longer. It's something you cultivate by doing things—often messily and often imperfectly.

That's why I now like to think of purpose as something you hone. It's a skill, rather than a singular destination. And like any skill, it improves through use and through trial and error. It improves through showing up and seeing what sticks, what stirs something inside you and what feels like it matters enough to keep returning to.

I often use the framework provided below when coaching people through this, which breaks down purpose into three powerful ingredients:

> "Purpose = Passion + Practice + Perseverance"

The first of these ingredients, passion, is the spark. It's the curiosity that pulls you in to focus on the topics and pursuits that make time feel elastic. You know this state when you're in it. It's when you can read for hours, talk endlessly or tinker with something long past the point of productivity, just because it feels good. Passion is often where purpose begins, but it can't end there.

Passion without practice is just a daydream. Practice is where you allow yourself to get messy. It's where you give yourself permission to be bad at something at first, to not have it all figured out, and to grow through doing rather than just through thinking. Back in chapter 1, I talked about the process for learning any skill, regardless of whether this is a language or a musical instrument. Happiness and purpose are no different. You don't need to be good at something to begin. You just need to begin.

And perseverance? That's what keeps you coming back over the long haul. Life will inevitably throw you off course. You will experience setbacks, detours and moments when you question it all. But perseverance is the quiet strength that reminds you to show up anyway—not for perfection but for progress, and not because it's easy but because it's worth it.

When you combine those three elements—when you follow what lights you up, commit to practising it even when it's hard and keep showing up with heart and grit—you'll find purpose begins to form. It will form slowly and subtly, but undeniably.

Another insightful tool that you can use to better understand your purpose is the Japanese concept of *ikigai*. Loosely translated as 'reason for being', more poetically it's what makes life feel worth living.

The Westernised interpretation of *ikigai* is often mapped into a Venn diagram with four overlapping circles that highlight:

1. what you love
2. what you're good at
3. what the world needs
4. what you can be paid for.

As shown in the following figure (overleaf), in the middle, where all four circles overlap, is your *ikigai*—your sweet spot.

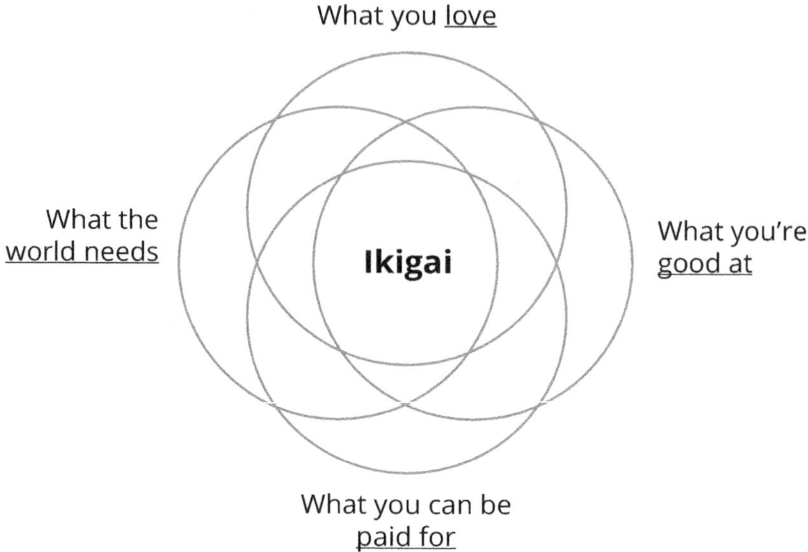

***Finding your* ikigai**

Now, is this model perfect? No. In truth, *ikigai* is a far more nuanced concept in its original cultural context, and boiling it down to a four-part diagram risks oversimplifying it. But what I do like about it is that it gives you a lens to start reflecting. It invites questions that matter, such as:

- 'What lights me up?'
- 'What am I naturally gifted at?'
- 'What do I deeply care about?'
- 'How might I contribute in a way that feels meaningful and sustainable?'

These aren't small questions, but they're worth asking—even if your answers change and evolve over time (which they will).

And that brings me to a deeper truth about purpose: it's not static. Just as your vision is permitted to change, so too is your sense of purpose. Your purpose in your 20s might be different from your purpose in your 40s. That doesn't mean you were wrong in your 20s; it means you're human. You're allowed to evolve. What matters is that you keep listening, keep responding and keep showing up for what matters now, in this current chapter of your life.

The following figure outlines the ways goals, purpose and vision interact. It also highlights which elements are more stable through your life and which are more prone to change.

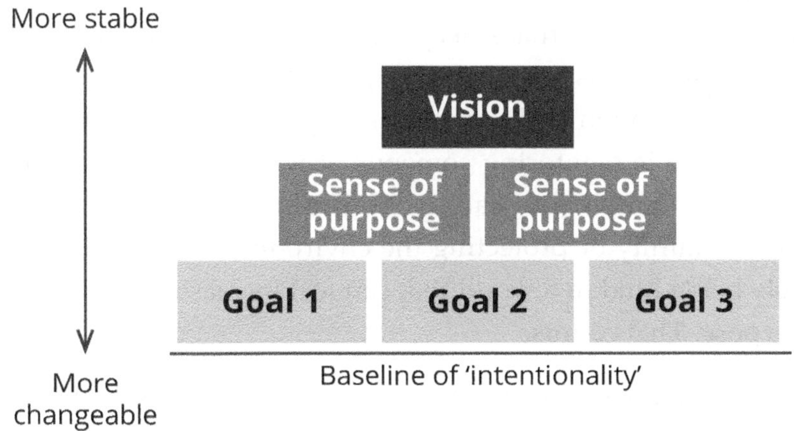

Goals, purpose and vision: Stability versus changeability

Viktor Frankl, the psychiatrist and Holocaust survivor whose work on meaning and purpose has influenced generations, wrote, 'Life is never made unbearable by circumstances, but only by lack of meaning and purpose'. Frankl observed that the people who endured unimaginable suffering in concentration camps were often those who had a reason, however small, to hold on. They had a sense of purpose—perhaps a loved one they hoped to see again or a belief in something beyond the present pain. That insight wasn't abstract. It was visceral. Survival, even in the worst conditions, was tethered to meaning.

Now, most of us will never face circumstances anywhere near that extreme. But the principle still holds. Purpose doesn't erase pain or struggle; it helps you navigate through it. It's not a shield from hard times, but it is a compass when you're in them.

Which brings me back to you. You might not know your 'big purpose' right now. That sweeping, all-caps reason for your existence might still evade you. And that's okay. You don't need to know it. What you can start with is your 'little purpose'. You can focus on the way you bring intention and meaning into your everyday life. Maybe this purpose is mentoring someone at work. Maybe it's cooking meals that nourish your family. Maybe it's showing up for your local community or protecting the environment or creating art or simply being kind in a world that can feel increasingly harsh. That is purpose. That counts.

And when in doubt? Focus on contribution. Ask yourself, 'How can I be of service today?' Not in a self-sacrificial way, but in a way that expands you, lifts others and leaves a little more good in the world than you found this morning.

Don't worry about getting it all 'right'. You're not trying to produce a mission statement here. You're learning to tune in, to pay attention, to what calls you. Purpose is rarely shouted. More often, it's whispered. Your job is to listen.

Reflection and application

Here are a handful of reflection questions to help you begin connecting with your personal sense of purpose. Remember — you're not looking for 'right' answers here. You're looking for honest ones. Ask yourself:

- 'When have I felt most alive?'
- 'What activities make me lose track of time?'
- 'Who do I admire and why?'
- 'What kind of impact do I want to have in my corner of the world?'
- 'What problems or causes tug at my heart?'
- 'What would I still care about deeply, even if I wasn't paid or praised for it?'

Intentionality: Living like you mean it

If vision is where you're heading and purpose is why you show up for the journey, intentionality is how you move through the world. It's the act of choosing your steps with clarity, care and presence rather than letting life sweep you along on autopilot.

And let's be honest with each other: autopilot is very tempting. It's easy to get swept up in the rhythm of daily life. The alarm goes off. The emails start. The meetings pile up. Dinner needs to be made. Bills need to be paid. The laundry needs folding, again. And before you know it, another week has passed and you're not quite sure how you got from Monday to Friday.

Living intentionally doesn't mean rejecting those day-to-day realities. It simply means not sleepwalking through them. It means showing up for your life with your eyes open, your hands on the wheel and your heart engaged. It means asking, 'What am I doing?' and, more importantly, 'Why am I doing it?' Intentionality is the antidote to drifting, and the bridge between knowing what matters and actually living like it matters.

One of the most common things I hear from people, especially those who are beginning to do the inner work of defining their values, vision and purpose, is that they want to live a life that feels aligned but they keep falling back into old patterns. They know what they care about. They know what kind of life they want. But they feel like they're still in the passenger seat watching the days pass them by, waiting for the right moment to really start.

Here's the truth: the right moment rarely shows up dressed in perfection. You will always have a messy kitchen, a half-finished to-do list or a part of you that wonders if you're really ready. Remember the hedonic treadmill I discussed back in chapter 1—the 'I'll be happy when … ' trap? It has a close sibling called the 'procrastination loop'. And it says, 'I'll do it when … ' This tendency encourages you to wait for the perfect timing, the perfect moment and the perfect conditions. But they never come. So you keep waiting.

Instead of waiting, intentionality invites you to start where you are, with what you have. In fact, that's one of the most freeing things about intentionality. It's not about perfection, and it's not about having it all figured out. It's about taking the smallest possible step in the direction of the life you want to live. It's deciding that how you spend your time, your energy and your attention is not a reaction to circumstance but a conscious response. It's a choice.

And like everything explored in this book, intentionality is a skill. It can be practiced, honed and strengthened. Doing so begins with awareness. If you don't know where your attention is going, you can't direct it somewhere more meaningful. You can't drive if you're not awake at the wheel.

And that's why everything we've covered so far matters:

- Your emotional intelligence helps you regulate and respond instead of react.
- Your introspection helps you pause and listen.
- Your mental retraining helps you challenge unhelpful patterns and focus on what's good and meaningful.
- Your self-knowledge helps you define what you care about.

All of that brings you here to the moment where you get to choose how to live, day by day. Intention, more than anything else, is about returning to yourself. It's the daily practice of realigning, coming back to what matters and remembering that your life is yours to shape, even if not every circumstance is in your control.

This is where you also need to draw a line between intentions and expectations:

- *Intentions are rooted in presence:* They say, 'I will show up for this moment with care and attention'.
- *Expectations are rooted in control:* They say, 'This moment needs to go exactly how I imagined it or I'll feel like a failure'.

Notice the difference? Intentions are flexible while expectations are rigid. Intentions are about the *how*. Expectations fixate on the *outcome*.

And if life has taught me one thing repeatedly it's that outcomes are never guaranteed. Circumstances shift, people change and plans unravel. But when you live with intention, you're no longer defined by whether life follows your script. You're defined by the integrity of your response. You're guided by your inner compass, not by the conditions of life.

To return to the road trip analogy (and I know I'm hammering it home), when you're living unintentionally, you will feel confined to the passenger seats of life. Life is moving, but you're not the one steering. Sometimes it will feel even worse than that, and like you're not even in the car. While you're still standing on the sidewalk, everyone else seems to have a plan, a destination and a map. You're still trying to figure out which way's forward.

Intentionality, when combined with vision and purpose, is your way of changing this and getting back into the driver's seat of life. It's your way of taking responsibility for your life and for your happiness. No-one else is coming to write your story. It's your pen, your hand and your pages. It's your responsibility and opportunity to do something with the finite and fleeting amount of time you have available to you in this life. So, please, don't let life and time pass you by. Choose to live with more intentionality.

And the beauty of intentionality is that you can choose it in every and any moment. You can pause right now and ask yourself:

- 'Am I being who I want to be?'
- 'Am I choosing how I show up?'
- 'Am I directing this moment or drifting through it?'

You don't need to overhaul your entire life to live intentionally. You just need to begin with the next right action. Above all, you need to give yourself permission to live intentionally and imperfectly. You won't always get it right. You'll forget. You'll slip back into old habits. And that's okay. What matters is returning, again and again, to what matters most.

Intentional living is a practice, a commitment and an ongoing skill. It's a choice to live like you mean it.

Reflection and application

Here are some simple ways to start practising intentionality today:

- *Start your day with a one-line intention:* Before checking your phone or diving into your inbox, take a breath and ask, 'What do I want to bring to today? Kindness? Focus? Patience? Presence?' Choose one and anchor yourself to it.
- *Create space to pause:* Use micro-moments throughout the day — for example, between meetings, before meals or while brushing your teeth. During these moments, ask yourself, 'Am I aligned right now? Am I being intentional?'
- *Reflect regularly:* At the end of your week, journal or simply reflect. Ask yourself, 'Where did I live in alignment with my vision and sense of purpose this week? Where did I drift?' Answer without judgement, and try to allow yourself to simply notice what answers come up for you.
- *Design your environment with intention:* The cues around you shape your habits. If you want to read more, put the book on your pillow. If you want to move more, lay out your running shoes. Your environment can be your ally. If you decide that part of living more intentionally involves exercising more regularly, for example, set up your home and living space to facilitate that.

Leading your life of happiness

So here you are. At the end of a chapter that's about not just happiness but also authorship, ownership and creating a life that feels like yours. And maybe, for the first time in a long time, you're starting to feel like you're in the driver's seat—not because every answer has been handed to you but because you've learned how to ask better questions. You've clarified where you want to go (your vision), why it matters (your purpose) and how you want to move through life (your intentionality).

This is no small thing. In fact, it's one of the bravest things you can do in a world that constantly tries to tell you who you should be, what you should want and how you should live. To instead pause and ask yourself, 'But what do I want? What matters to me? What do I want this life of mine to stand for?' takes courage. But this process of reflecting and choosing, redirecting when you've strayed and living on purpose rather than out of habit is how you build a meaningful life. That's how you turn happiness from a vague, elusive wish into something intentional, grounded and real.

By now you've seen that this chapter, and this skill of directing your life, doesn't live in isolation. It's the culmination of everything we've practised together so far:

- Your emotional intelligence helps you understand and honour how you feel.
- Your introspection gives you the space and tools to listen to yourself.
- Your mental retraining helps you reframe and refocus your mindset.

- Your self-knowledge, including your values, your strengths and your love languages, gives you clarity about who you are.

And now, with this final skill, you're invited to take everything you've uncovered and do something with it:

- Define a vision that feels inspiring and true.
- Create a purpose that brings you meaning and energy.
- Approach each day with intentionality.

This chapter isn't a full stop but a hand-off. It's a baton passed back to you because, ultimately, this is your story to write. As we move ever closer to the end of our time together in this book, I encourage you to step into the role of leading your life and of actively cultivating a life of happiness. And as you step into that role, I hope you do so with compassion for your past, clarity in your present and curiosity for what's still to come.

The following quote from Howard Thurman (shared by Gil Bailie in an account of their 1974 conversation) has travelled with me through times of doubt and growth:

> Don't ask what the world needs. Ask yourself what makes you come alive, and go do that, because what the world needs is people who have come alive.

You may not feel like you've fully found what makes you feel alive, what makes you feel most aligned and what makes you feel deeply happy, yet. That's okay. Remember the lessons from the opening chapters of this book—happiness is less of a destination and more of a path you walk, one meaningful, intentional step at a time.

I hope that this chapter has sparked something in you. Perhaps it's sparked the beginnings of a vision for what a happy life looks like on your terms, a feeling of possibility and a sense that you already have everything you need inside of you. Whatever this chapter has sparked within you, I hope you hold onto it. I hope you nurture it. I hope you let it guide you forward.

It's your time now. The pen is in your hand. And the rest of your life is waiting to be written. I hope you do so with vision, purpose and intentionality.

Conclusion: Every ending holds a new beginning

Certain ideas settle into you and shape how you see the world. They're the kind of truths that don't just land in your mind but also echo in your chest. One of those truths that has fundamentally changed the way I approach life is this: endings are never just endings. Every closing chapter carries within it the seed of a new one. The end of winter gives way to the first signs of spring. The end of the night opens into dawn. A goodbye can become the opening to a deeper connection, a shift in direction or a rediscovery of self.

So, yes, we've reached the end. But I hope that in many ways, this is only your beginning:

- The beginning of you being more intentional with your happiness.
- The beginning of you recognising that happiness is a skill set you can learn, grow and share.
- The beginning of a ripple effect that could stretch far beyond you and change lives you may never even meet.

At the end of the day, this book was never just about happiness as a feeling. It was about happiness as a force for good.

Let's pause and remember what you've just done. You've read a book on happiness. That's no small thing. And you haven't read a fluffy, vague, unicorns-and-rainbows kind of book on happiness either. You've spent time with the science of happiness. You've explored five of the most impactful, evidence-backed skills that help people build happier, more fulfilling lives. And, most importantly, you've looked inward, reflected and engaged. You've done the work.

You've learned how to build your emotional intelligence so that you can understand and regulate your emotions more effectively. You've learned how to turn inward through introspection and use tools such as journaling and meditation to uncover your patterns, navigate your inner world and foster clarity. You've practised retraining your brain by cultivating gratitude, managing expectations and shifting perspective. And you've challenged your negative bias and started shaping a more balanced perspective of how you see yourself and the world around you. You've done the brave work of getting to know yourself deeply—including your values, strengths, and unique way of expressing and receiving love. And you've wrapped all of that into an intentional life—a life lived with direction, with clarity of purpose and with intentional daily actions that align with the vision you hold for yourself.

These five skills don't promise perfection. They won't make you immune to hardship or erase every bad day. But they do equip you with something more powerful than perfection: the ability to keep going, to reset, to reflect and to rise again. They help you become the kind of person who doesn't wait for happiness to arrive like a delivery at the door but instead builds it from within. And like any skill worth learning, they take practice.

Remember: happiness wasn't ever a destination for you to arrive at. It's more like learning an instrument. You're going to have days when your fingers feel clumsy on the strings, when you forget the chords, when it's easier to put the guitar down than keep strumming. But the only way to get better is to keep practising; to show up again and again not just for the music, but for what the music brings out in you.

The same goes for your happiness skills. These skills will rust if you neglect them. They'll fade if you forget to use them. So revisit them. Reread this book. Reflect on what landed for you, and what you want to try again. Think of this book not as a one-time read but as a resource—a guidebook you can return to whenever life gets loud, confusing or off track.

Because the world needs people like you. More than ever, we need people who know how to regulate their emotions instead of being consumed by them. We need people who have learned to look inward before reacting outward, and who've trained their minds to notice beauty, possibility and potential—not just problems. We need people who are deeply aligned with who they are, who live with purpose and who show up each day with intention.

In short, we need more people who have learned the skills and science of happiness. And we need this not just for their own benefit, but because happiness is contagious—literally. As mentioned back in chapter 1, research by Nicholas Christakis and James Fowler has shown that happiness spreads through social networks up to three degrees of separation. That means if you become happier, your friend is more likely to become happier, and your friend's friend. The ripple effect of your joy could reach people you'll never meet.

In fact, the same Christakis and Fowler study found that having a happy friend who lives within a mile increases your chances of being happy by about 25 per cent. Even seeing someone smile in a coffee shop line can subtly boost your mood. Emotional contagion is real. And when it comes to happiness, it's incredibly powerful.

Of course, the same is true for stress, anxiety, division and despair. We live in a world where unhappiness is often centre stage. Turn on the news and you'll see headlines crafted to spike fear and outrage. Scroll social media and you'll be bombarded with highlight reels and encouraged to doomscroll in equal measure. Walk into many workplaces or social groups and you'll hear more complaining than celebrating. As traditional media has always maintained, 'If it bleeds, it leads'. And what leads, shapes culture.

But here's where you come in. You don't have to buy into it. You don't have to be another echo of disconnection or cynicism. You can be the one who shows up differently, the one who listens more, thanks more, laughs more, forgives more and sees the good more. You can be the one who quietly, steadily shifts the tide—starting with yourself and rippling outward.

That's why I wrote this book. I wrote it not only to help you feel a little better about life (though I genuinely hope you do), but also because I believe deeply in your potential to play a part in making the world a happier place.

I've dedicated my life's work to a mission that's simple to say but massive in scope: to grow global happiness. It's a vision I can't achieve alone, and I don't intend to. I believe it will be achieved one person at a time, one skill at a time and one ripple at a time. It will be achieved through people like you reading books like this, practising what you've learned, and then sharing it with the people around you.

And that sharing doesn't have to be dramatic. You don't need to launch a movement or stand on a stage (though if that's your jam, go for it). Maybe, for example, you:

- lend this book to a friend who's been struggling (or, better yet, buy copies as gifts for the people you care most about in your life)
- model emotional intelligence for your kids
- bring more intention to your morning coffee and start your day with clarity
- thank someone who never expected to be thanked.

And maybe, because of your actions, someone else does the same for someone else. And on it goes.

As I've been writing and talking about this book, I've said that it was not written in Vegas and it doesn't follow Vegas rules. What happens in this book should not stay in this book. You've learned life-changing skills. Don't keep them to yourself. Use them, live them and share them. Let them shape the way you walk through the world.

At this point, I know you might feel inspired but also a little overwhelmed. You might be thinking, *Who am I to make a difference?* or *What impact could I possibly have?* If so, remember:

- You don't have to be perfect. You just have to be willing.
- You don't have to change the world. You just have to change your world.
- From there, the ripple will do the rest.

So please, keep learning these skills. Keep practising them. Keep growing.

If this book has sparked something in you—if you want to dive deeper into mastering not just these five skills but the many other skills and frameworks that support a happy and fulfilling life—I'd love for you to continue that journey with us at the BU Happiness College, and you'll find more details about how to do that on the page 195.

For now, thank you for showing up for yourself, for the people you love and for the world we share.

I hope you go out there and create the kind of life and the kind of ripple effect that only you can make by practising the skills and science of happiness, and by being you.

Acknowledgements

I believe no project is a self-made success. This book is the result of countless mentors who have shaped my thinking, clients who have entrusted me with their happiness development and loved ones who have supported me—especially my wife, Siobhann.

This book is dedicated to them, because, without them, it wouldn't be the book that it is and I wouldn't be the man that I am.

About Declan Edwards

Declan Edwards is a happiness philosopher, author and speaker, and the founder of BU Happiness College—a social enterprise dedicated to helping people and workplaces thrive through the skills and science of happiness.

Blending the insights of positive psychology with down-to-earth coaching and storytelling, Declan has spent the past decade helping thousands of people build more fulfilling lives. He has appeared in publications such as *The Newcastle Herald, ABC News, The Daily Telegraph* and *Psychology Today*. He's also a TEDx speaker, a guest lecturer and advisor, and an emerging thought leader in the field of happiness science.

Declan is passionate about making the science of happiness simple, practical and human. He believes happiness isn't about perfection but progress—and that the more people who learn these skills, the more we can collectively shift toward a world that's kinder, more connected and more hopeful.

When he's not coaching or writing, you'll find him enjoying quality time with his wife, his son and their two dogs, playing basketball or soaking up slow mornings in nature.

This book is his invitation to you to be curious, to grow your happiness skills, and to play your part in spreading a ripple effect that makes the world a happier and better place.

About BU Happiness College

BU Happiness College was founded on one simple but impactful belief: the world becomes a better place when people are empowered to be themselves and when they are equipped with the skills to live happier, more fulfilling lives.

We exist to help individuals grow their personal happiness, support workplaces to thrive and ultimately contribute to a ripple effect of happiness that extends far beyond ourselves. Whether it's in the home, the office or the broader community, happiness changes everything—and we're here to help people learn how to make it happen.

The 'BU' in BU Happiness College stands for 'Be You', a message that sits at the heart of everything we do—because the greatest gift you can give the world is to show up as your true self, and live a life that feels aligned with who you really are.

We're not about shallow positivity or one-size-fits-all advice. We offer practical, evidence-based tools drawn from the science of positive psychology and human wellbeing. And we provide these tools in ways that are warm, real and deeply human. From self-paced learning to one-on-one coaching and workplace programs, everything we offer is designed to help people build real skills for real happiness.

We're proud to have members and graduates in five countries and growing. Our work has been recognised with multiple awards and featured in numerous publications, and continues to receive consistently high happiness ratings from the people who matter most—our members, clients and graduates. More than the accolades, what matters most to us is the impact we see in the lives of our members and clients. We are consistently inspired by the way they flourish, grow and begin to spread the ripple effect of happiness into the world around them.

At BU, you'll find more than just education; you'll find a community that genuinely cares. You'll find a place to learn, grow, be challenged, be supported and, most importantly, be yourself.

Continue your happiness and personal growth journey

You can continue your happiness journey with the following:

- Keep learning by listening to our podcast *How To Be Happy*—available on Spotify, Apple Podcasts or wherever you get your podcasts.
- Learn more about the skills and science of happiness via our range of free resources, including our Happiness Scorecard and the 'Skills and Science of Happiness' microclass, available at buhappinesscollege.com/free-resources.

- Continue practicing the skills taught in the book by enrolling in our six-week course 'The Certificate of Happiness Studies' via buhappinesscollege.com/certificate. Use the code BOOK to save 25 per cent.
- Discover all 75 skills of happiness taught in our self-paced e-learning program 'The Happiness Blueprint', available via buhappinesscollege.com/happiness-blueprint
- Explore our one-on-one happiness coaching, guided by our incredible team of Personal Happiness Coaches. Find out more at buhappinesscollege.com/coaching. Use the code BOOK100 for $100 off your first session.
- Bring happiness to your organisation through our workplace happiness services, including staff training and keynote speaking. Go to declanedwards.com.au for more information.

References and further reading

Introduction

Australian Bureau of Statistics (2023), 'Two in five Australians have experienced a mental disorder'. Retrieved from https://www.abs.gov.au/media-centre/media-releases/two-five-australians-have-experienced-mental-disorder.

Black Dog Institute (2022), 'Positive psychology fact sheet'. Retrieved from https://www.blackdoginstitute.org.au/wp-content/uploads/2022/06/Positive-psychology-fact-sheet.pdf.

Camfield, L & Esposito, L (2014), 'A cross-country analysis of perceived economic status and life satisfaction in high-income countries', *World Development*, 59(1), 212–223.

Conklin, CN (2015), 'The origins of the pursuit of happiness', *Washington University Jurisprudence Review*, 7(2), 195–262.

Gable, SL & Haidt, J (2005), 'What (and why) is positive psychology?', *Review of General Psychology*, 9(2), 103–110.

Gallup (2022), 'World unhappier, more stressed out than ever'. Retrieved from https://news.gallup.com/poll/394025/world-unhappier-stressed-ever.aspx.

Gallup (2025), *State of the World's Emotional Health 2025*. Accessed via https://www.gallup.com/analytics/349280/state-of-worlds-emotional-health.aspx.

Google (2020), 'Year in Search 2020'. Retrieved from https://trends.google.com/trends/yis/2020/US/; https://x.com/GoogleTrends/status/1336750591184269312.

Harrison, S (2024), *New Happy: Getting Happiness Right in a World That's Got It Wrong*, Penguin Random House.

Kentley Insights (2025), *Psychologists and Counselors Market Size & Growth—2025 Global Report*. Retrieved from https://www.kentleyinsights.com/psychologists-counselors-market-size/.

Lyubomirsky, S, Sheldon, KM & Schkade, D (2005), 'Pursuing happiness: The architecture of sustainable change', *Review of General Psychology*, 9(2), 111–131.

National Institute of Mental Health (2022), 'Mental illness'. Retrieved from https://www.nimh.nih.gov/health/statistics/mental-illness.

Ortynsky, SN, Farag, M & Mou, H (2023), 'Wellbeing budgets in New Zealand and Canada: What can municipalities learn?' Institute on Municipal Finance & Governance. Retrieved from https://imfg.org/uploads/628/imfg_talk_wellbeing_budgets_stephanie_ortynsky_nov_23_2023.pdf.

Parks, AC & Schueller, SM (2014), *The Wiley Blackwell Handbook of Positive Psychological Interventions*, Wiley Blackwell.

Research and Markets (2023), *Personal Development Market Size, Share & Trends Analysis Report by Instrument 2023–2030*. Retrieved from https://www.researchandmarkets.com/reports/5595847/personal-development-market-size-share-and-trends.

Seligman, MEP & Csikszentmihalyi, M (2000), 'Positive psychology: An introduction. *American Psychologist*, 55(1), 5–14.

University of Cambridge (2015), 'Practice really does make perfect. Retrieved from https://www.cam.ac.uk/research/news/practice-really-does-make-perfect.

Chapter 1

Achor, S (2010), *The Happiness Advantage: The Seven Principles of Positive Psychology that Fuel Success and Performance at Work*, Crown Currency.

Ackerman, CE (2018), 'What are positive emotions in psychology? (+list & examples)', PositivePsychology.com.

Bharti, NK, et al (2024), 'Income and wealth inequality in India, 1922–2023: The rise of the billionaire Raj', World Inequality Lab.

Csikszentmihalyi, M (1990), *Flow: The Psychology of Optimal Experience*, Harper & Row.

Deci, EL & Ryan, RM (2006), 'Hedonia, eudaimonia, and well-being: An introduction', *Journal of Happiness Studies*, 9(1), 1–11.

Diener, E & Seligman, MEP (2002), 'Very happy people', *Psychological Science*, 13(1), 81–84.

Diener, E, Lucas, RE & Scollon, CN (2006), 'Beyond the hedonic treadmill: Revising the adaptation theory of well-being', *American Psychologist*, 61(4), 305–314.

Fowler, JH & Christakis, NA (2008), 'Dynamic spread of happiness in a large social network: Longitudinal analysis over 20 years in the Framingham Heart Study', *BMJ*, 337, a2338.

Fredrickson, BL (2001), 'The role of positive emotions in positive psychology: The broaden-and-build theory of positive emotions', *American Psychologist*, 56(3), 218–226.

Kern, ML, et al (2014), 'A multidimensional approach to measuring well-being in students: Application of the PERMA framework', *The Journal of Positive Psychology*, 10(3), 262–271.

Lyubomirsky, S, Sheldon, KM & Schkade, D (2005), 'Pursuing happiness: The architecture of sustainable change', *Review of General Psychology*, 9(2), 111–131.

Lyubomirsky, S (2008), *The How of Happiness: A Scientific Approach to Getting the Life You Want*, Penguin Press.

Ryff, CD & Singer, BH (2008), 'Know thyself and become what you are: A eudaimonic approach to psychological well-being', *Journal of Happiness Studies*, 9(1), 13–39.

Santos, L (2020), The science of well-being [Online course]. Yale University.

Seligman, MEP (2011). *Flourish: A Visionary New Understanding of Happiness and Well-being*, Free Press.

Willcox, G (1982), 'The Feeling Wheel: A tool for expanding awareness of emotions and increasing spontaneity and intimacy', *Transactional Analysis Journal*, 12(4), 274–276.

World Happiness Report (2025), 'Caring and sharing: Global analysis of happiness and kindness'. Retrieved from https://worldhappiness.report/ed/2025/caring-and-sharing-global-analysis-of-happiness-and-kindness/.

Chapter 2

Brackett, MA (2019), *Permission to Feel: The Power of Emotional Intelligence to Achieve Well-Being and Success*, Celadon Books.

Bryant, FB & Veroff, J (2007), *Savoring: A New Model of Positive Experience*, Lawrence Erlbaum Associates Publishers.

Cohen, S & Wills, TA (1985), 'Stress, social support, and the buffering hypothesis', *Psychological Bulletin*, 98(2), 310–357.

Creswell, JD, et al (2007), 'Neural correlates of dispositional mindfulness during affect labeling', *Psychosomatic Medicine*, 69(6), 560–565.

David, S (2016), *Emotional agility: Get Unstuck, Embrace Change, and Thrive in Work and Life*, Avery Publishing Group.

Goleman, D (1995), *Emotional Intelligence: Why It Can Matter More Than IQ*, Bantam Books.

Gross, JJ & Levenson, RW (1997), 'Hiding feelings: The acute effects of inhibiting negative and positive emotion', *Journal of Abnormal Psychology*, 106(1), 95–103.

Harris, R (2008), *The Happiness Trap: How to Stop Struggling and Start Living*. Trumpeter Books.

Holiday, R (2014), *The Obstacle is the Way: The Timeless Art of Turning Trials into Triumph*, Portfolio.

Hölzel, BK, et al (2011), Mindfulness practice leads to increases in regional brain gray matter density', *Psychiatry Research: Neuroimaging*, 191(1), 36–43.

Jose, PE, Lim, BT & Bryant, FB (2012), 'Does savoring increase happiness? A daily diary study', *The Journal of Positive Psychology*, 7(3), 176–187.

Kabat-Zinn, J (1990), *Full Catastrophe Living: Using the Wisdom of Your Body and Mind to Face Stress, Pain and Illness*, Delacorte.

Lieberman, MD, et al (2007), 'Putting feelings into words: Affect labeling disrupts amygdala activity in response to affective stimuli', *Psychological Science*, 18(5), 421–428.

Tugade, MM & Fredrickson, BL (2004), 'Resilient individuals use positive emotions to bounce back from negative emotional experiences', *Journal of Personality and Social Psychology*, 86(2), 320–333.

Vago, DR & Silbersweig, DA (2012), 'Self-awareness, self-regulation, and self-transcendence (S-ART): A framework for understanding the neurobiological mechanisms of mindfulness', *Frontiers in Human Neuroscience*, 6, 296.

Wyatt, Z (2024), 'The dark side of #positivevibes: Understanding toxic positivity in modern culture', *Psychiatry and Behavioral Health*, 3(1), 1–6.

Chapter 3

Alter, A (2017), *Irresistible: The Rise of Addictive Technology and the Business of Keeping Us Hooked*, Penguin Press.

American Psychological Association (2019), 'Mindfulness meditation: A research-proven way to reduce stress'. Retrieved from https://www.apa.org/topics/mindfulness/meditation.

Baikie, KA & Wilhelm, K (2005), 'Emotional and physical health benefits of expressive writing', *Advances in Psychiatric Treatment*, 11(5), 338–346.

Bell, R, Mieth, L & Buchner, A (2022), 'Coping with high advertising exposure: A source-monitoring perspective', *Cognitive Research: Principles and Implications*, 7, Article 82.

Davidson, RJ, et al (2003), 'Alterations in brain and immune function produced by mindfulness meditation', *Psychosomatic Medicine*, 65(4), 564–570.

Simms, A & Murray, L (2024), 'How many ads do you see?', *The Ecologist*.

Hodgkinson, GP, Langan-Fox, J & Sadler-Smith, E (2008), 'Intuition: A fundamental bridging construct in the behavioural sciences', *British Journal of Psychology*, 99(1), 1–27.

Kabat-Zinn, J (2003), 'Mindfulness-based interventions in context: Past, present, and future', *Clinical Psychology: Science and Practice*, 10(2), 144–156.

Liu, M & Ren, S (2018), 'Moderating effect of emotional intelligence on the relationship between rumination and anxiety', *Current Psychology*, 37(1), 272–279.

Pearson, J (2024), 'Go with your gut: The science and psychology behind our sense of intuition', *The Guardian*.

Silvia, PJ & Phillips, AG (2013), 'Self-awareness without awareness? Implicit self-focused attention and behavioral self-regulation', *Self and Identity*, 12(2), 114–127.

Siteefy (2025), 'How many ads do we see a day?'. Retrieved from https://siteefy.com/how-many-ads-do-we-see-a-day.

Tang, YY, Hölzel, BK & Posner, MI (2015), 'The neuroscience of mindfulness meditation', *Nature Reviews Neuroscience*, 16(4), 213–225.

University of Rochester Medical Center (nd), 'Journaling for Emotional Wellness'. Retrieved from https://www.urmc.rochester.edu/encyclopedia/content.aspx?ContentID=4552&ContentTypeID=1.

WindowStill (2023), 'The Surprising number of advertisements we're exposed to daily'. Retrieved from https://www.windowstill.com/the-surprising-number-of-advertisements-were-exposed-to-daily/posts/.

Chapter 4

Bartlett, MY, & DeSteno, D (2006), 'Gratitude and prosocial behavior: Helping when it costs you', *Psychological Science*, 17(4), 319–325.

Davidson, RJ & Begley, S (2012), *The Emotional Life of Your Brain: How Its Unique Patterns Affect the Way You Think, Feel, and Live—and How You Can Change Them*, Avery Publishing Group.

Emmons, RA & McCullough, ME (2003), 'Counting blessings versus burdens: An experimental investigation of gratitude and subjective well-being in daily life', Journal of Personality and Social Psychology, 84(2), 377–389.

Fox, GR, et al (2015), 'Neural correlates of gratitude', *Frontiers in Psychology*, 6, 1491.

Fredrickson, BL (2004), 'Gratitude, like other positive emotions, broadens and builds', in Emmons, RA & McCullough, ME (eds), *The Psychology of Gratitude*, Oxford University Press.

Gilbert, DT (2006), *Stumbling on Happiness*, Knopf.

Hanson, R (2013), *Hardwiring Happiness: The New Brain Science of Contentment, Calm, and Confidence*, Harmony Books.

Kahneman, D (2011), *Thinking, Fast and Slow*, Farrar, Straus and Giroux.

Killingsworth, MA & Gilbert, DT (2010), 'A wandering mind is an unhappy mind', *Science*, 330(6006), 932.

Kini, P, et al (2016), 'The effects of gratitude expression on neural activity', *NeuroImage*, 128, 1–10.

Kurtz, JL (2008), 'Looking to the future to appreciate the present: The benefits of perceived temporal scarcity', *Psychological Science*, 19(12), 1238–1241.

Lambert, NM, et al (2009), 'A changed perspective: How gratitude can affect coherence through positive reframing', *The Journal of Positive Psychology*, 4(6), 461–470.

McCullough, ME, Emmons, RA & Tsang, J (2002), 'The grateful disposition: A conceptual and empirical topography', *Journal of Personality and Social Psychology*, 82(1), 112–127.

Rozin, P & Royzman, EB (2001), 'Negativity bias, negativity dominance, and contagion', *Personality and Social Psychology Review*, 5(4), 296–320.

Sapolsky, RM (2017), *Behave: The Biology of Humans at Our Best and Worst*, Penguin Press.

Steindl-Rast, D (2013), 'Want to be happy? Be grateful' [video], TED Conferences.

Wood, AM, Froh, JJ & Geraghty, AWA (2010), 'Gratitude and well-being: A review and theoretical integration', *Clinical Psychology Review*, 30(7), 890–905.

Chapter 5

Ware, B (2012), *The Top Five Regrets of the Dying: A Life Transformed by the Dearly Departing*, Hay House.

Chapman, G (2015), *The 5 Love Languages: The Secret to Love that Lasts*, updated ed, Northfield Publishing.

Harzer, C & Ruch, W (2016), 'Your strengths are calling: Preliminary results of a web-based strengths intervention to increase calling', *Journal of Happiness Studies: An Interdisciplinary Forum on Subjective Well-Being*, 17(6), 2237–2256.

Holt-Lunstad, J, Smith, TB & Layton, JB (2010), Social relationships and mortality risk: A meta-analytic review, *PLOS Medicine*, 7(7), e1000316.

Keyes, CLM (2002), 'The mental health continuum: From languishing to flourishing in life', *Journal of Health and Social Behavior*, 43(2), 207–222.

Peterson, C & Seligman, MEP (2004), *Character Strengths and Virtues: A Handbook and Classification*, Oxford University Press; American Psychological Association.

Reis, HT & Aron, A (2008), 'Love: What is it, why does it matter, and how does it operate?', *Perspectives on Psychological Science*, 3(1), 80–86.

Sheldon, KM & Elliot, AJ (1999), 'Goal striving, need satisfaction, and longitudinal well-being: The self-concordance model', *Journal of Personality and Social Psychology*, 76(3), 482–497

VIA Institute on Character (nd), 'Take the free VIA Survey'. Retrieved from https://www.viacharacter.org/.

Watkins, PC, et al (2003), 'Gratitude and happiness: Development of a measure of gratitude, and relationships with subjective well-being', *Social Behavior and Personality: An International Journal*, 31(5), 431–452.

Chapter 6

Baumeister, RF & Vohs, KD (2002), 'The pursuit of meaningfulness in life', in Snyder, CR & Lopez, SJ (eds), *Handbook of Positive Psychology*, Oxford University Press.

Deci, EL & Ryan, RM (2008), 'Facilitating optimal motivation and psychological well-being across life's domains', *Canadian Psychology/ Psychologie canadienne*, 49(1), 14–23.

Delle Fave, A, Massimini, F & Bassi, M (2011), *Psychological Selection and Optimal Experience across Cultures: Social Empowerment through Personal Growth*, Springer Science + Business Media.

Emmons, RA (2003), 'Personal goals, life meaning, and virtue: Wellsprings of a positive life', in Keyes, CLM & Haidt, J (eds), *Flourishing: Positive Psychology and the Life Well-Lived*, American Psychological Association.

García, H & Miralles, F (2017), *Ikigai: The Japanese Secret to a Long and Happy Life*, Penguin Books.

Gollwitzer, PM (1999), 'Implementation intentions: Strong effects of simple plans', *American Psychologist*, 54(7), 493–503.

Kashdan, TB & McKnight, PE (2009), 'Origins of purpose in life: Refining our understanding of a life well lived, *Psihologijske Teme*, 18(2), 303–316.

Ryan, RM, & Deci, EL (2000), 'Self-determination theory and the facilitation of intrinsic motivation, social development, and well-being', *American Psychologist*, 55(1), 68–78.

Steger, MF (2012), 'Making meaning in life', *Psychological Inquiry*, 23(4), 381–385. https://doi.org/10.1080/1047840X.2012.720832.

Wong, PTP (2012), 'Toward a dual-systems model of what makes life worth living', in Wong, PTP (ed), *The Human Quest for Meaning: Theories, Research, and Applications*, 2nd ed, Routledge.

Conclusion

Christakis, NA & Fowler, JH (2009), *Connected: The Surprising Power of our Social Networks and How They Shape Our Lives*, Little, Brown Spark.

Haidt, J (2006), *The Happiness Hypothesis: Finding Modern Truth in Ancient Wisdom*, Basic Books.

Printed and bound by CPI Group (UK) Ltd, Croydon, CR0 4YY

14/06/2026

14899569-0002